FUN WITH THE GREEK MYTHS

John Ollivier

BNR Press • Port Clinton, Ohio

Copyright ©1989
All rights reserved
Published by BNR Press
132 East Second Street, Port Clinton, Ohio 43452
(419) 734-2422
Manufactured in the United States of America
International Standard Book Number: 0-931960-25-8 (soft bound)
0-931960-26-6 (hard bound)

CHAPTERS

The Genesis of the Gods............................	1
The Strange Children of the Night.............	8
Mythological Monsters................................	10
Descendants of Mother Earth....................	12
The Reign of the Titans..............................	19
The Off-spring of Zeus...............................	24
The Olympians..	35
Olympian Escapades..................................	44
Olympian Wrath...	60
Olympian Gratitude.....................................	79
Humans Beware..	82
Olympian Response to Prayer...................	85
Olympian Retribution..................................	96
Fate...	99
Greek Heroes..	106
Mythological Birds......................................	119
The Argonauts..	134
A Love Story...	141
A Tragedy...	144
The Trojan War..	148
Problems and Solutions.............................	167
The Why of Seasons.................................	175
Centaurs...	178
The Thorn of Thebes.................................	180
Some Final Stories....................................	195

INDEX OF POEMS

Achilles' Heel..	157
Admetus and Alcestis...................................	104
Amazons, The..	159
Apple of Discord..	150
Ares, the Mean God.....................................	33
Argus and the Peacock................................	48
Athena, Goddess of Wisdom.....................	25
Beware of Greeks...	163
Big and Little Bears, The.............................	51
Cadmus' Family Curse.................................	192
Calydonian Boar Hunt, The.........................	100
Cassandra...	162
Castor and Pollux..	89
Chaos...	2
Chariot of the Sun, The................................	92
Charon..	7
Cheiron...	179
Conclusion..	201
Cretan Bull Story, A......................................	112
Cronus and Zeus...	21
Crows, Nightengales, Swallows................	125
Daedalus and Icarus.....................................	120
Daughter's Betrayal, A.................................	129

Daughters of Danaus, The	76
Echidna	11
Echo	55
Epigoni	190
Erysichthon	78
Flood, The	174
Foolish Vote of Midas, The	83
From Olympus to Rome	43
Goddess of Dawn, The	34
Great God Pan, The	200
Grey Ladies, The	13
Helle and Phrixus	135
Hephaestus	29
Heracles	108
Hermes and His Tricks	27
How Things Came To Be	4
Inhospitable Hospitality	116
Iphigenia	154
Kingdoms of the Universe, The	41
Laurel Tree, The	58
Lethe, River of Forgetfulness	197
Lightening Bolt Makers	31
Midas the Macedonian King	80
Musical Contest, A	63
Mythological Brats	9

Naming A City	195
Night and Day	6
Niobe's Pride	69
Oedipus Rex	146
Origin of the Frog, The	95
Origin of the Nemean Games	188
Origin of the Spider, The	61
Pandora	98
Perithous and Theseus	117
Persephone	176
Perseus	171
Phineus and the Harpies	137
Poor Little Absyrtus	140
Psyche and Cupid	142
Punishment of Sisyphus, The	73
Pygmalion	86
Ring of Polycrates	102
Seven Against Thebes	183
Sinis, the Pinebinder	115
Some Titans	45
Strange Children of Gaea	15
Tantalus	66
Titan War, The	37
Uncatchable Fox, The	168
Uranus and Gaea	17
Why Crows Changed Colors	132

THE GENESIS OF THE GODS

Way back in the beginning of time, long before there was anything at all, there existed only Chaos. This most ancient of all the gods was the only god that was. In fact, there was no other being. All was Chaos.

Somehow, Eros, the beautiful and primeval personification of love sprang into being. He became the uniting influence responsible, in every way, for bringing the conflicting elements of this Chaos to the harmony and order that was necessary for the rest of creation to come into being.

CHAOS

Things began with Chaos,
And we haven't come too far.
Till love was made by Eros,
There wasn't even a star.

We should learn from this
What love can do.
Even confusion
It can subdue.

Under the unifying and creative influence of Eros there rose out of Chaos the beautiful goddess, Eurynome - the goddess of all. She looked around and saw that she had nothing to stand on so she divided the sea from the sky. The movement of her graceful body created a wind by which she became pregnant. In due time she begot Ophion, a very great and monstrous serpent.

Then in her creative power, she laid a universal egg which the serpent hatched and all things came into being.

Eurynome and Ophion lived together happily on Mount Olympus until she banished him into the netherworld for bragging that he was the creator of the universe.

HOW THINGS CAME TO BE

Long before stars came to be
And long before the deep blue sea,
At the very beginning of time
When all was muck and ugly slime,
A god name Chaos was the king
But there really wasn't anything.

But what is a king without a queen?
So goddess Eurynome appeared on the scene.
And what is it that she begot?
A serpent, Ophion, believe it or not!
It hatched an egg the goddess laid.
All things sprang forth without further aid.

Eurynome then met with Chaos. And Nyx (Night) and Erebus came into being. Then Nyx and Erebus met in love and there appeared Aether (Light) and Hemera (Day).

Charon, the aged and dirty ferryman who transports souls across the river Styx as they enter Tartarus, the realm of the dead, was also born of this union.

Charon always demanded a fee. Thus a silver coin was placed on the tongue of every Greek corpse.

A honey-cake was also buried with the corpse in order to feed Cerberus, Charon's three headed dog.

Night and Day now dwell at the brazen gates of Tartarus. Their pattern of activity is always the same, for when one leaves, the other enters. One always follows the other.

NIGHT AND DAY

When Chaos and Eurynome
Met in love,
Nyx and Erebus
Were the fruit thereof.

Nyx and Erebus
Then slipped away,
And they begot
Both Night and Day.

They dwell in the land
Where departed grieve,
As one does enter,
The other does leave.

They have a brother,
Charon, by name.
He has achieved
No little fame.

Listen and I
Will tell you the story.
It is quite grim
And rather gory.

CHARON

Charon was a river boat captain
Who ferried the River Styx.
If dead had not a coin on tongue,
They were in a dreadful fix.

Cerberus was his three-headed dog.
He, too, demanded his mite.
If dead brought not a honey-cake,
They'd feel his awful bite.

THE STRANGE CHILDREN OF THE NIGHT

Nyx alone begot many strange children. Their very names are ominous: Doom, Death, Fate, Sleep, Dreams, Blame, Revenge, Woe, and Deceit, to mention but a few. Eris, the goddess of Strife and Discord, was the last of her very frightful children.

Without a mate, Eris became the mother of her own ugly brood: Toil, Forgetfulness, Famine, Sorrow, Battle, Lying, Murder, Fighting, Quarrel, Lawlessness, and others.

So hideous were these children of Night and Eris they were placed within a chest and the lid was quickly closed to keep them in. These hideous beings did not roam the earth until Pandora foolishly opened the box.

MYTHOLOGICAL BRATS

Nix alone
Begot children strange,
But her baby Eris
Was most deranged.

The children of Eris
Were ugly and brutal.
To list all their crimes
Would, indeed, be futile.

So ugly were they
They were put in a box.
And there they would stay
Until Pandora unlocks.

MYTHOLOGICAL MONSTERS

Night again met with Chaos in love. Two children were born of this union, Gaea (Mother Earth) and Tartarus (Netherworld). Then Gaea and Tartarus met in love and Begot the monster serpent called Typhon. The very mountains fell beneath his weight. On his shoulders were 100 heads.

Typhon embraced Echidna, the daughter of the winged horse, Crysaor, who with the strange Pegasus, had sprung from the gorgon Medusa's blood.

Echidna begot many of the famous monsters we read about in Greek Mythology. She begot Cerberus (the three-headed dog of Charon), and the venomous Hydra who grew two additional heads each time one head was lopped off. She begot the Chimaera, the Nemean Lion that Heracles killed, Orthus, the two-headed hound of Geryon, the Eagle which nightly consumed the liver of Prometheus, the Sphinx that killed all who were unable to solve his riddle, and the Cochis Dragon that guarded the golden fleece.

ECHIDNA

Echidna, prolific breeder
Of monsters large and small,
Her off-spring frightens reader,
But Typhon worst of all.

If monsters would have never been,
Heroes there would not be.
What separates the boys from men
Is the opportunity.

Heracles needed the lion
As Oedipus needed the Sphinx.
Pegasus would still be flyin'
Without Bellerophon, me thinks.

DESCENDANTS OF MOTHER EARTH

Gaea also had unfathered offspring, Pontus (Sea) and Uranus (Sky). She begot Actaeus, Cecrops, and Cranaus in this manner. These last three children were called Autochthons which means they sprang from the earth. Their lower body was that of a dragon.

Gaea then met with Pontus and soon begot two daughters, Ceto and Eurybia, and three sons, Phorcys, Nereus, and Thaumus. Ceto married her brother Phorcys and by him begot a curious brood. Their first issue was collectively called the Graeae, so called because they had grey hair at their birth.

They had only one eye and one tooth between the three of them. When it was needed, they passed it around. If the eye or tooth was not needed, it was kept in a coffin. Their names where Pemphredo, Enyo, and Deino.

These three sisters played an important role in the tales of the Greek hero, Perseus, the son of Zeus and Danae. Perseus had been tricked by his mother's suitor into accepting the challenge of cutting off Medusa's head. Only the Graeae knew where Medusa lived and they wouldn't tell.

The following story reveals how Perseus pried out of the Graeae their privileged information.

THE GREY LADIES

The Graeae were three ladies grey,
With one eye, one tooth between them.
When Perseus sought where Medusa dwelt,
Not one of them would tell him.

So he took the eye they passed around,
And the tooth that went between them.
And they had to swear on the River Styx,
Before he would return them.

So they squealed on poor Medusa,
Who was soon to lose her head.
They now can see and eat again,
But the gorgon, Medusa, is dead.

The gorgons were a second trinity of daughters born to Ceto and Phorcys. Their names were Sthenno, Medusa, and Euryale.

They had wings, brazen claws and enormous teeth. If one looked at them, one was turned immediately into stone.

Ladon was another of the curious offspring of Ceto and Phorcys. He was a remarkable dragon that could talk. He guarded the golden apples. Hera placed him in the sky as a constellation to reward him for his service.

Thoosa was the final daughter of Ceto and Phorcys. She married the sea-god, Poseidon and begot the one-eyed giant, Polyphemus.

Phorcys also had another daughter by the foreboding goddess, Hecate. This beautiful and charming daughter was Scylla. But when Poseidon was attracted to Scylla because of her beauty, Amphitrite, the daughter of Nereus and wife of Poseidon, turned Scylla into a sea monster with twelve feet and six mouths. She was then placed upon a rock between Sicily and Italy. There this once beautiful maiden, now made monster, frightened sailors as they approached and caused many shipwrecks.

THE STRANGE CHILDREN OF GAEA

Gaea and Pontus
Begot quite a brood.
Some were quite gentle,
Others quite rude.

Monsters and Harpies,
And Gorgons and Furies,
Serpents and beasts
That cause lots of worries.

To Uranus, the Titans
And Cyclops she bore,
And giants as big
As dinosaurs.

Uranus was the second son of Gaea and by union with her begot the mighty Titans. They were twelve in number, Ocean, Coeus, Crius, Hyperion, Iapetus, Theia, Rhea, Themis, Mnemosyne, the mother of the Muses, Phoebe, Tethys, to whom was entrusted the education of Hera, and Cronus the last of the Titans.

Gaea then bore to Uranus three Cyclops, the one-eyed giants who assisted in making thunderbolts. Their names were: Brontes, Arges, and Steropes. Gaea then bore the Hecatoncheires, monsters with fifty heads and one hundred arms. Their names were Cottus, Briareus, and Gyes.

Uranus was upset with his monster children and hid them far beneath the surface of the earth. This, of course, upset their mother no little. She made a sickle of stone in her anger and induced her youngest son, Cronus, to kill his own father.

With his dying breath Uranus put a curse upon his son foretelling that one day Cronus' own son would bring about the death of his father. This curse weighed heavily upon Cronus, so much so that he ate his children at their birth, so that the prophetic promise of their grandfather would never be fulfilled.

URANUS AND GAEA

Offspring of Chaos
Were Heaven and Earth,
Called Uranus and Gaea
The day of their birth.

They begot monsters
Hideous to behold,
And one-eyed Cyclops,
What a household!

Many headed dragons,
With hundreds of hands,
They were much more
Than Uranus could stand.

He was proud of his Titans,
But the monsters he hid,
Until Gaea their mother,
His plans would forbid.

Gaea asked Cronus
To kill his own father,
Cause he considered his kin
Too much of a bother.

Uranus predicted
As his life was bedimmed,
Cronus' own son
One day would kill him.

From the blood of Uranus
The Furies sprang forth,
As from the blood of Medusa
Came Pegasus the horse.

With Father in Hades
And Cronus now king,
Uranus' curse
Made him eat his offspring.

THE REIGN OF THE TITANS

With the fall of Uranus the Titans proclaimed Cronus their king. He chose Rhea, his sister, to be his wife and queen.

In due time Rhea gave birth to six children. All were destined to be Olympian gods. Their names were, Hestia, Demeter, Hera, Hades, Poseidon and Zeus.

But mindful of his father's curse, Cronus ate each of his children at birth. After he had eaten the first five, Rhea, their mother, was quite upset and sought the counsel of Gaea.

Gaea went to Crete where Zeus was born. She neatly wrapped a rock in swaddling cloths and gave it to Cronus who quickly swallowed it, thinking it to be Zeus, his newborn son.

Ida and Adrasteia, daughters of King Melisseus, nursed the infant Zeus with milk from a goat named Almatheia. This goat was later rewarded by Zeus who placed her in the heavens as the constellation Capricorn.

Zeus broke off the goat's horn and gave it to Ida and Adrasteia as a horn of plenty, cornucopia. It would always be filled with whatever they desired, and when emptied, it would be magically refilled.

This cornucopia was later given to Achelous, a river god. Lesser deities called Curetes were summoned to beat drums and cymbals at Zeus' birth so that the infant cries of the newly born would not be heard by Cronus.

When Zeus grew up he met the goddess Metis, the wisest of Ocean's daughters. He expressed his concern about his swallowed brothers and sisters. She mixed a concoction which Zeus was to give in a surreptitious way to his aged father.

When he drank the potion out came the rock. It was followed by the brothers and sisters of Zeus.

CRONUS AND ZEUS

Uranus was proud
Of his Titans so brave,
But the Cyclops he hid
In a rocky cave.

This angered Gaea;
Her monsters she missed.
She plotted a crime
That involved quite a risk.

She ordered Cronus
Her young Titan son
To kill his father
And the deed was done.

He slaughtered Uranus
With a sickle of stone
So his monster brothers
Now could come home.

Uranus cursed Cronus
In dying hate
And foretold for his son
A similar fate.

From the blood of Uranus
The Furies sprang.
Those who kill kinsmen
They forever harangue.

Then Cronus became
The Titan king
And sought a wife
To wear his ring.

His sister Rhea
Became his queen.
This brought joy
To the Titan scene.

But soon the marriage
Hit the skids,
When Cronus began
To eat his kids.

One would knock him off
He felt
So he kept them safe
Beneath his belt.

Woeful Rhea
Then cleaned his clock;
It was not Zeus he ate
But a diapered rock.

Almathea's milk
Nursed little Zeus
Who grew up to cook
His father's goose.

With a potion from Metis
Things went amuck.
Old Cronus felt
The urge to upchuck.

Out came Zeus'
Brothers and sisters
Without even disturbing
Their father's whiskers.

Almathea's reward?
She lost her horn
And was tossed into heaven
As Capricorn.

Her horn was given
To a god of the river
With the promise the given
Would return to the giver.

Thus we have
The Cornucopia
Which makes of this earth
A real Utopia.

It'll always be filled
With food and drink.
That's heaven on earth
At least most people think.

THE OFF-SPRING OF ZEUS

Metis was the first wife of Zeus. She was the very wise daughter of Ocean. When she was carrying her first child, Gaea informed Zeus that Metis would first bear him a girl, but later she would bear him a son and the son would eventually overthrow him.

To prevent the fulfillment of this prophesy Zeus swallowed Metis who was pregnant with his infant daughter. When the time arrived for the birth of the child, Zeus had a terrible headache which nothing could cure, until at last, Hephaestus struck Zeus on the head with an axe. Out jumped the full grown Athena, the goddess of wisdom.

ATHENA, GODDESS OF WISDOM

One day Zeus had a headache,
The pain was quite severe.
Nothing seemed to cure it,
Till Vulcan's axe appeared.

He split the head wide open,
And a goddess made debut.
It was divine Athena,
Who would teach Zeus all he knew.

This story has a moral,
And it is plain to see.
To get the gift of wisdom
Headaches must always be.

Hermes was the son of Zeus by Maia. As a child he was most precocious. On the very day of his birth Hermes slipped out of his crib and stole the cows of Apollo. Shortly after this he invented the lyre which he constructed from cow gut and the shell of a tortoise.

When Apollo discovered the theft of his cows, he picked up Hermes and carried him to Mount Olympus where he formally accused him of crime. Hermes finally confessed but told Zeus that he took the cows that he might offer sacrifice to the twelve gods of Olympus.

"And who is the twelfth?" he was asked by Zeus. "Your servant, sir." he replied.

Zeus was so delighted with this little ingenious godling that he welcomed him to Olympus.

To placate Apollo for his missing cows Hermes presented the lyre to Apollo as a gift. Apollo graciously forgave him and cherished the lyre.

Hermes was employed on Olympus as a messenger of the gods.

HERMES AND HIS TRICKS

Hermes was a messenger
At Zeus' beck and whim.
He sped from heaven to the earth
And then sped back again.

He led the dead to Hades
Their journey was quite quick.
He angered and amused the gods
On each he played a trick.

He stole the cows of Apollo
Backing them up so they wouldn't tell,
Then appeased him with the lyre he made
From gut and tortoise shell.

He charmed the gods of Olympus
By his pranks and by his mirth.
They rejoiced that he was one of them,
A godling from his birth.

Hephaestus was the son of Hera and Zeus. He was such a weakling at his birth that his mother cast him out of Olympus. He fell into the sea but was rescued by Thetis and Eurynome who raised him to become a craftsman of great skills. He made beautiful ornaments for the Olympian gods.

When Hera saw the fine jewelry he made she brought him back to Mount Olympus where she set up for him a fine blacksmith shop. His marriage to Aphrodite, the goddess of love, was arranged by Zeus. Aphrodite was never a faithful wife.

Hephaestus was cast from heaven once again when he foolishly rebuked his father for hanging Hera by her wrists from the heavens. He landed on the Island of Lemnos and broke both legs in the fall. He has since been called the lame god. Once again he was reconciled with Zeus and practiced his artful skill on Mount Olympus. He made the aegis for Zeus, the Chariot of the Sun for Helios, the bows of Apollo, the helmet for Hades, and the trident for Poseidon. His masterpiece, however was Pandora, the first woman.

HEPHAESTUS OR VULCAN

Vulcan was a son of Zeus,
A craftsman of iron and steel.
He made most things for all the gods,
And they always got a deal.

He was a workaholic god,
Making Zeus' bolts of thunder.
So Venus messed around a lot
And is it any wonder.

Bows were forged for Apollo,
A helmet for King Hades.
He fashioned the chariot of the sun,
And Pandora, the first of ladies.

The Cyclops assisted Vulcan in the execution of his esteemed craftsmanship. They were the one-eyed giants disdained by their father, Uranus, who cast them into jail far beneath the surface of the earth. Cronus also doomed them to this same fate.

It was Zeus who set them free and, in gratitude, they aided him in overthrowing the Titans. The thunderbolts of Zeus were made by the Cyclops in their workshop deep in the earth beneath Mount Etna.

LIGHTNING BOLT MAKERS

The Cyclops were great giants
With but a single eye.
They were jailed by their father,
Uranus, meaning sky.

Cronus, too, rejected them
But Zeus did set them free.
Thus to show their gratitude
His friend they'd always be.

They assist the great god Vulcan
When before his forge he stands.
In all his artful labors
They lend their skillful hands.

They make the bolts of thunder,
That Zeus is wont to throw.
They work beneath Mount Etna,
From which they seldom go.

Some call this mount volcanic
As smoke breaks through its crest,
But there is no need to panic,
It's the forge put to its test.

Ares was the son of Zeus and Hera. He was the god of War. Like his sister, Eris, he loved battle for its own sake. He delighted in the slaughter of men. Even though he was an Olympian god, his fellow immortals despised him.

He was not courageous, but rather cowardly. He was not even a skillful warrior and was often defeated by others. On one occasion the gigantic sons of Aloeus conquered him and imprisoned him in a brazen vessel for thirteen months. He was finally freed by Hermes. The vulture was his favorite bird.

An extra-marital affair with fair Aphrodite, the unfaithful wife of Hephaestus, proved most embarrassing. The smith god had caught them in an invisible net he had fashioned and invited the gods and goddesses to view them in their lustful deed. The gods anxiously arrived, but the goddesses declined the invitation.

ARES, THE MEAN GOD

Ares was a mean god,
As mean as mean can be.
And even as mean as he was,
He was even more cowardly.

When Diomedes wounded him
He fled to Olympus crying.
A tiny, little, simple wound!
You'd think that he was dying.

He was hated by his fellow gods,
Except his sister, Strife,
And his secret lover, Venus,
Who was really Vulcan's wife.

But Vulcan got his vengeance,
When the Sun made him aware.
He trapped them in their lustful deed,
By forging an invisible lair.

He then called the gods together,
This spectacle to see.
They came and laughed, but not their wives
Who declined in modesty.

THE GODDESS OF DAWN

Aurora was the goddess of dawn
Those who met her always yawned.
She put to flight the morning star
Revealing the sun was not too far.
As she passed a fresh breeze blew
Announcing that the day was new.

THE OLYMPIANS

Zeus never forgave his father for the way he had treated his children, Zeus' brothers and sisters. When Zeus grew up he called his brothers and sisters to a meeting on Mount Olympus.

He informed them that he intended to overthrow Cronus and his fellow Titans. He promised great rewards to anyone who would help him in his task.

The River goddess, Styx, even though herself a daughter of a Titan, Ocean, and the wife of Pallas, son of the Titan, Crius, pledged uncompromising support. She promised the assistance of her four powerful children: Bia (Force), Cratos (Strength), Nike (Victory) and Zelus (Emulation).

As a reward Zeus conferred upon her the eternal honor of having her name used thereafter by all of the gods in taking oaths. Henceforth such oaths would be inviolable. Her four children were ever after the attendants of Zeus in battle. With much promised assistance Zeus set out to overthrow Cronus. All of the Titans, except Ocean, took the part of Cronus.

Two of the four sons of Iapetus assisted Cronus. They were Atlas and Menoetius. His other two sons, Prometheus and Epimetheus sided with Zeus.

The Titan War began. The Titans entrenched themselves in the Othrys Mountains while Zeus encamped on Mount Olympus. The fierce battle took place on the plains between. After ten years of fighting, the war was still a stalemate.

Zeus went to Gaea to seek counsel. Gaea disliked Cronus ever since he had imprisoned her sons the Cyclops. Gaea told Zeus to free the Cyclops from their subterranean jail and enlist their help.

The Olympian god descended to the netherworld and slew Campe, the dragon that guarded the Cyclops. When they were freed they fought on the side of Zeus. With the thunderbolts of the Cyclops and the strength of the Hecatoncheires the Titans were quickly defeated and cast into Tartarus where they still dwell.

THE TITAN WAR

As time did pass
And Zeus grew up,
A Titan War
Would soon erupt.

Zeus would depose
His father, Cronus,
And become the sovereign
As a bonus.

A decree for help
His name affixed.
It quickly came
From the River Styx.

She came to Zeus
In Olympian tower,
And pledged her offspring's
Invincible power.

This deed became
Her path to fame.
Henceforth all oaths
Would bear her name.

The war began.
Ten years it lasted.
A tie! And both
Were flabbergasted.

The advice of Gaea
Was sought by Zeus.
She counseled:
"Let the Cyclops loose."

They hated Cronus
Who jailed them.
Their one desire:
"Impale him."

With the Hecatoncheires
They won the war.
And Zeus became
The sovereign Tsar.

Down to Tartarus
Titans were cast,
To be there as long
As time would last.

But the Titan Atlas
Who helped his kin
Must hold up the sky
Till time does end.

The Titans were imprisoned in Tartarus and the Hecatoncheires were appointed their jailers forever. Atlas was forced to hold up the sky in punishment for his part in the war.

Zeus became the supreme ruler. He appointed Poseidon to rule the sea and Hades to govern the realm of the dead.

Zeus kept the realms of heaven and earth for himself. He ruled from Mount Olympus.

THE KINGDOMS OF THE UNIVERSE

Zeus divided
The world in three,
Heaven and hell
And the deep blue sea.

Pluto ruled
The realm of the dead.
Poseidon ruled
The sea, it's said.

For himself
Zeus kept the rest.
I really think
He got the best.

Zeus was now the ruler of the gods who lived on Mount Olympus. These gods were immortal and although human in form, their powers far exceeded men.

They did have limitations in knowledge, however, and they had corporal wants and human affections.

The name of the Olympians in Greek and Latin are as given: Zeus (Jupiter); Hera (Juno); Athena (Minerva); Apollo in both languages; His sister Artemis (Diana); Ares (Mars); Hephaestus (Vulcan); Hermes (Mercury); Aphrodite (Venus); Hestia (Vestia); Hebe (Juventas); and Demeter (Ceres).

Hera was the sister and wife of Zeus. Athena was his daughter by Metis. Apollo and Aretmis were his children by Leto. Hephaestus and Ares were sons by Hera. Aphrodite was his daughter by Dione and Hermes was his son by Maia.

Hestia and Demeter were the sisters of Zeus.

FROM OLYMPUS TO ROME

The Romans took their gods from Greeks
But often changed the name.
They also took their many bleeps,
But loved them just the same.

Zeus in Rome was Jupiter,
While Hera was called Juno.
Apollo kept his lovely name,
But Hades was known as Pluto.

Poseidon renamed was Neptune.
Hephaestus was called Vulcan.
Artemis became Diana
When worshiped by the Roman.

Athena became Minerva,
Goddess of Wisdom and Arts.
Fair Aphrodite was Venus,
As she played with Roman hearts.

Eros renamed was Cupid.
Ares was war-like Mars.
Hermes renamed was Mercury,
Who sped among the stars.

That leaves us only Hestia
Of the Olympian mighty gods.
She became the Virgin Vesta,
When on Roman soil she trods.

OLYMPIAN ESCAPADES

Zeus was the supreme god in Greek Mythology. We have seen something of his origin. Now we must look at his adult life. He had but one wife, Hera, but many, many lovers. Thus many of the stories in Greek Mythology are but accounts of his escapades in origin, circumstance, and consequence.

The famous Greek heroes in battle with men and monsters are mostly his descendants. Apollo and Artemis are his offsprings by Leto. Heracles was his son by Alcmene, Perseus his son by Danae, Theseus his distant descendant.

Many of the myths originate in their plot with the almost uncontrollable jealousy of Hera. And Zeus certainly gave her cause to be jealous.

One of his first affairs was with Mnemosyne, the goddess of memory. She gave birth to the nine Muses that are so famous in literature. The Muse of epic poetry was Calliope; Cleio was the Muse of history; Erato was the Muse of love songs; Euterpe was the Muse of lyric poems; Melpomene was the Muse of tragedy; Polyhymnia was the Muse of song; Thalia was the Muse of comedy; Terpsichore was the Muse of dance; and Urania was the Muse of astrology.

SOME TITANS

Poseidon ousted Ocean,
After the Titan War.
When Titans fell from favor,
No longer were they adored.

Atlas, too, was punished
By Olympians on high.
He received a heavy sentence.
He must hold up the sky.

But Mnemosyne was loved by Zeus,
And begot for him a little Muse,
Nine of them to be exact.
This is not myth, but certain fact.

Another of Zeus' many affairs was with Io, the beautiful daughter of the river god, Inachus. Zeus tried to conceal his lusts by covering himself with a cloud. But unexplained clouds always made Hera suspicious. She quickly came to earth and ordered the cloud away. But Zeus, anticipating the wiles of Hera, had turned Io into a beautiful white heifer and denied any misconduct. Hera did not believe a word of it.

She complimented Zeus on the beauty of the heifer and asked that he make her a gift of it. Thus tricked by the clever and jealous Hera, Zeus reluctantly turned Io over to his wife. She gave the cow to Argus to guard for her. Argus was most suited for this task for he had a hundred eyes and he could sleep with one eye at a time.

Zeus seemed helpless as he beheld poor Io's misery. At last he went to Hermes, the cleverest of the gods, and told him he must find a way to do away with Argus.

Hermes visited the hundred-eyed guard and began to tell him stories, very dull stories. So dull were the stories that after a time all the eyes of Argus fell asleep. The messenger of Zeus then killed Argus and set the beloved Io free.

Hera took the eyes of Argus and placed them in the tail of her favorite bird, the proud peacock.

Io fled and was restored to human form by Zeus. She then begot her son, Epaphus.

ARGUS AND THE PEACOCK

Argus had
a hundred eyes,
Quite a tool
For one who spies.

And this he did
Most zealously,
For Juno's fits
of jealously.

He guarded Io
Now made cow.
Her affair with Zeus
Caused quite a row.

Saddened at
Poor Io's plight
Zeus sent Hermes
With the speed of light.

He told tales to Argus
Dull and deep,
And eye by eye,
He fell asleep.

In fact, he breathed
His final breath,
The poor old guy
Was bored to death.

So Juno plucked
Those hundred eyes
That for her
Had so often spied.

She put them on
Her favorite bird,
It's called a peacock,
So I've heard.

The peacock's known
For its pride
Exhibited in
Its very stride,

Ugly feet,
But what a tail!
Reaching perfection
In the male.

It's the eyes that make
This bird so vain.
It all happened
During Juno's reign.

The unfaithfulness of Zeus with Io was certainly not a singular event. Nor was Hera's jealousy. This is brought out most clearly in the story of Callisto. Callisto was the daughter of the infamous King Lycaon who had been punished by Zeus when he served his divine dinner guest human flesh. His punishment was deserved, but his daughter suffered a far worse fate and she was entirely innocent.

Zeus saw Callisto hunting in the company of Artemis and fell in love with her. This, of course, angered Hera and in her anger she turned Callisto into a bear after she had given birth to Zeus's son, Arcas.

When the boy had grown up and was out hunting, Hera brought Callisto before him, intending to have Arcas shoot his own mother, without knowing it, of course. But at that moment Zeus snatched both son and mother away and placed them in the heavens as the constellation Big and Little Bear. Hera was enraged at this honor bestowed upon her rivals. She then persuaded the god of the sea to forbid the Bear Stars ever to descend into the oceans to rest like the other stars.

They alone among all the constellations never set below the horizons.

THE BIG AND LITTLE BEARS

The Arcadian nymph, Callisto,
Once was loved by Zeus.
He tried to hide it from his wife,
Telling lover to vamoose.

But Juno was all-seeing,
As mistress bore a son.
When she gave birth to Arcas,
Her troubles had just begun.

"I'll take away your beauty,
Which so enticed my mate.
You'll crawl upon the earth a bear,
And tragedy await."

Dark black hair soon covered her,
Her hands grew into claws.
Where once had been such pretty lips,
There was now a pair of jaws.

A bear afraid of other bears,
Fleeing wolf and hound.
A huntress in fear of hunters,
Walking four feet on the ground.

Arcas one day espied her,
As he was hunting game.
He lifted bow and arrow,
And took his deadly aim.

What son thought was aggression,
Was a mother seeking love.
So when he shot his arrow,
Zeus acted from above.

Before the deed of matricide,
As arrow sped through air,
Zeus made each a constellation,
THE BIG AND LITTLE BEAR.

Juno was enraged to see,
Her rivals in the sky,
Exulted in her heavens,
Admired by every eye.

Who would fear her godly wrath,
If sin won such a prize.
She could not undo what Zeus had one,
Still she couldn't compromise.

So Juno went to Ocean,
Who listened to her pleas.
"Do not permit the Bear Stars,
To rest within your seas."

They are the only constellations,
That do not descend to rest.
They remain constantly in heaven,
To which mariners attest.

There was a beautiful nymph who was an attendant to Queen Juno. Her name was Echo. She was quite a chatterbox and talked incessantly. This proved most inconvenient for Juno, for she could no longer sneak up to spy of Zeus. He always heard her coming due to the constant and noisy chatter of her attendant. It was easy for Zeus to conceal his amorous affairs.

Exasperated Juno placed a spell on Echo. Henceforth she may never speak first. She may only repeat what others have said, and then, only the last word. Humiliated and deeply hurt, Echo fled into the mountains to hide her shame. One can still hear her there repeating what others have first said.

ECHO

Echo was a beautiful nymph
Fond of woods and hills.
She only had one failing
Constant chatter gave her thrills.

Attendant to Queen Juno,
She talked incessantly.
Zeus always heard them coming
And sped off secretly.

So Juno placed a spell on her
Which made the nymph see red.
She could only repeat the last word
That others first had said.

She ran off to the mountains,
There to hide her shame.
It's there you still can hear her.
What you say, she'll say the same.

Zeus was not the only god that was fickle in love; nor was he the only god that had many affairs with humans. Poseidon was far more promiscuous. Apollo ran a very close second.

On one occasion the love that Apollo offered was spurned by the beautiful nymph named Daphne. The laurel wreath that Apollo wears on his head can be traced to this rejection. The story is told as follows.

Cupid was the playful son of Aphrodite and Ares. He shot arrows of love into the hearts of the young and love became irresistible. This is why he is so often depicted with the bow and arrow.

Apollo, the great archer god, made fun of Cupid with his undersized bow. This so irritated Cupid that he sought revenge. He shot an arrow of love for Daphne into the heart of Apollo, but into Daphne he shot an arrow of disdain and indifference for Apollo.

Daphne was passionately pursued by Apollo in his lust for her, but in her disdain for him she fled into the woods. Apollo continued to pursue and when just about to catch her she prayed to her father, the river god Peneius, to spare her such an indignity. At that moment Peneius changed his daughter into a laurel tree.

Bewildered at what he saw, Apollo broke off the branches and made a wreath for his head. If he could not have Daphne, he could at least have a lasting memento of her.

THE LAUREL TREE

There were two gods
With bow and arrows.
Cupid shot hearts,
Apollo shot sparrows.

Apollo despised
The little runt,
So Cupid decided
To pull a stunt.

An arrow of love
For lovely nymph, Daphne,
Pierced the heart of Apollo
From Cupid, the Crafty.

But into the nymph
The runt shot disdain.
So Apollo pursued
Poor Daphne in vain.

When just about
to catch his love,
Daphne sent up
Prayers above.

"River god, father,
Please help me."
He did.
She became a laurel tree.

Since such a thing
He could not wed,
He plucked off the branches
And placed on his head.

And so we have
The laurel wreath,
To make amends
For Apollo's grief.

OLYMPIAN WRATH

Not only were the gods similar to men in their need and quest for love, but so often they reflected in their deeds the faults and the weaknesses of men.

The passion of anger was not wanting in the divine disposition. It especially flared up when humans competed with the gods in their divine skills. This is evidenced most clearly in the delightful story of Arachne and Athena.

As Hephaestus was the craftsman of the gods, Athena was the weaver. Her work was unapproachable for its fineness of thread and its beauty of pattern.

One can imagine her outrage when a peasant girl named Arachne declared her human weaving to be superior. The goddess challenged the upstart Arachne to a contest. Arachne accepted with joy.

Athena's work was worthy of the goddess. But Arachne's work was in no way inferior. But in her weaving she insulted the gods as she depicted their many illicit love affairs.

Athena was furious and turned the maiden Arachne into a spider that would weave forever.

THE ORIGIN OF THE SPIDER

Although she'd passed
The age of acne,
Neither wisdom nor reverence
Graced little Arachne.

She treated the gods
In utter jest,
Challenging even Athena
To a weaver's contest.

She mocked the gods
In the weaving she wove,
And incurred the wrath
Of haughty Jove.

Olympus upset with
This godless outsider,
Turned the upstart Arachne
Into a spider.

"You are a brilliant
Weaver, " they said.
"Now weave, you wretch,
An eternal web."

Not only was irate reaction to human competition a flaw among the female deities of Olympus, it was often exhibited among their male counterparts. We see this flaw in the reaction of Apollo to the musical skills of Marsyas.

Apollo, the god of the lyre, so belittled the flute and its master player, Marsyas, that Marsyas in desperation challenged Apollo to a contest. Apollo accepted only on the condition that the loser would be flayed.

The competition was close, but Apollo took an unfair advantage. He sang as he played and awed his listeners. Marsyas, of course, could not sing as he played the flute.

The story and its outcome is told in the following poem.

A MUSICAL CONTEST

Marsyas played
A lovely flute.
I mean by that
He could really toot.

Apollo played
The stringed lyre,
Which everyone
Who heard admired.

Apollo laughed
At Marsyas' flute,
Who didn't think
This very cute.

He challenged Apollo
To a test,
Let people judge
Which is best.

Marsyas played.
The people drooled.
Apollo didn't
Follow the rules.

As he played
He sang along.
In doing so
He awed the throng.

Marsyas couldn't
Pipe and sing.
One set of lips
Can't do such a thing.

The one who lost
Was flayed and skinned.
Now Marsyas has nothing
Where skin had been.

It would not be quite fair to depict the anger of the gods as only resulting from insane envy at the talents of creatures. At times their anger was more than justified. In the following stories of Tantalus, Niobe, Sisyphus, and Erysichthon we see the pitch of their anger when not given the proper respect.

Tantalus among mortals was the most favored by the gods. They permitted him to eat at their table and taste the ambrosia and nectar, the food and drink of the gods. They even honored Tantalus by accepting an invitation to dine in his palace. And how atrociously the gods were treated by their human host! He fed them human flesh. He boiled his own son, Pelops, and served him to the gods.

He was severely punished for such ill-treatment of divine guests. He was cast into Hades and tormented with insatiable hunger and thirst. Cold water and delicious fruit were placed just beyond his reach.

TANTALUS

Tantalus, a son of Zeus,
Was a favorite of the god.
Alone among all mortals,
He on Olympus trod.

He alone had tasted
Their ambrosia and nectar.
But soon he would discover
A god is a great corrector.

He invited the Olympians
To banquet in his house.
He should have served some royal food,
At least a well-cooked grouse.

But instead he served them Pelops,
His darling little son,
When in the kitchen over,
He finally was done.

Insulted by this mischievous deed,
The Olympian gods and ladies
Ordered their ungrateful cook
Into the depths of Hades.

It is there that you will find him
Suspended still, I think,
Just beyond the grasp of food
And beyond the grasp of drink.

You'll find him ever reaching,
But never realizing.
Thus we have a god-made word.
The word is TANTALIZING.

Not only were the Olympian gods jealous of their divine skills and talents, they were even more jealous of their divine honor.

When humans refused to worship them or to make the sacrificial offerings the Olympians demanded, the divine wrath quickly descended upon them. Witness this in the story of Niobe.

Niobe had been blessed by the gods. She was happily married to Amphion, a skilled musician, who was the king of Thebes. But she was a daughter of Tantalus, and his arrogance lived on in her. As her father sought to deceive the gods, she defied them openly.

She mocked her subjects for offering worship to Leto whose shrine was in Thebes. Leto was the mother of Apollo and Artemis. Leto had only two children while Niobe had seven sons and seven daughters. Why should Leto be worshiped and not her?

The following poem depicts the results of her arrogance.

NIOBE'S PRIDE

Niobe was a presumptuous broad,
The Queen of Thebes was she.
She mocked the goddess Leto
And wouldn't bend her knee.

"Why should this Titan be worshiped?
On what did she stake her claim?
She only had two children!
What right is that to fame?"

Seven times that number Niobe had,
Seven girls and seven boys.
Let her subjects worship her
And cease their Letonic noise.

Leto grew indignant
On her Cynthian mountain throne.
She summoned both her children
Who hurried to her home.

"Speech only delays her punishment."
Apollo said as she told her tale
He gathered with his sister Diana
Fourteen arrows that never fail.

The sons of Niobe were gaming
Outside the city gate.
Ismenos was the eldest
And the first to meet his fate.

Two younger sons were wrestling
As Apollo kept his oath.
He avenged his slighted mother
As one arrow pierced them both.

Six sons were quickly slain by him.
Ilioneus alone was left.
He begged the god to spare him
But an arrow came true and deft.

Amphion then slew himself;
His wife decried the slaughter
"Bereaved I am still richer than you
For I still have seven daughters."

The daughters were in mourning
What evil had been wrought.
Diana now got into the act
And each an arrow caught.

Niobe was reduced to tears
As her children's death she moaned.
Her husband, too, had killed himself
So Leto turned her into stone.

A fountain sprang from atop that stone
A tribute to her grief.
Her tears continue still to flow,
From pride there's no relief.

Let the haughty learn from this
The lesson of my tale.
If today you sing with pride,
Tomorrow you will wail.

The anger of the gods and the imaginative punishments they could devise in that anger are revealed in their dealings with Sisyphus, the arrogant king of Corinth.

One day Sisyphus saw a mighty eagle in the sky bearing a maiden to a nearby island. He realized the eagle was far more splendid than any mortal bird. When the river god Asopus came by hunting for his daughter, Aegina, whom he strongly suspected had been carried off by Zeus, Sisyphus revealed what he had seen, and thereby incurred the terrible wrath of the mighty Zeus.

As punishment Sisyphus was to be cast into Hades. The clever Sisyphus realized what would soon befall him. Thus he told his wife to deny him proper funeral rites. When in Hades he then convinced Pluto that he should permit him to return to earth to receive the proper burial rites from his wife. He would return to the realm of the dead as soon as this was done.

But once Sisyphus again walked in the land of the living he soon forgot his promise. When the gods finally forced Sisyphus into Hades, they devised an unusual punishment for him. He must roll a boulder up a hill, and when at the top, he must let it fall back to the bottom. The futility of this process must continue for all eternity.

THE PUNISHMENT OF SISYPHUS

The tale is told of Sisyphus,
Perhaps the cleverest of men,
Certainly the craftiest,
Who did the gods offend.

He outwitted Autolycus,
The greatest living thief.
He branded cattle neath their hooves,
And thus got back his beef.

He outsmarted even Hades,
The god of all that's scary.
When called into the netherworld,
He forbid his wife him bury.

He pleaded to return to earth,
For proper funeral rite,
Then refused to descend again,
Once he saw the earth's daylight.

When Zeus fled with Aegina,
River Asopus' daughter,
He squealed on this lustful god,
When he really hadn't oughter.

When finally forced to Hades,
The place that all despised.
He received this awful punishment,
The netherworld gods devised.

He was forced to roll a boulder
Up a hill so tall.
And when he almost reached the top,
He had to let it fall.

Down again he had to go,
To push infernal rock.
Again and again he must repeat,
Round Hades' timeless clock.

The dread of existentialism,
According to Camus,
Is clearly evidenced in this scene,
Known only by a few.

The dread they often talk about,
Is not Sisyphus pushing stone.
It's trudging vainly down the hill,
That gnaws him to the bone.

The Danaids are among the prominent sufferers in Hades. They are the fifty daughters of Danaus, a descendant of Io.

These fifty daughters married the fifty sons of Aegyptus, the brother of Danaus. Danaus despised his nephews and asked his lovely daughters to kill them after the marriage. He gave each daughter a dagger to perform the deadly deed.

On the very night of their marriage all but one of Danaus' daughters destroyed their unsuspecting spouse. Only Hypermnestra could not bring herself to execute such a hideous crime.

Forty nine of Danaus' daughters are now punished in Hades with a punishment as senseless as their crime. They must carry water in a leaky jar and eternally stoop to refill it.

THE DAUGHTERS OF DANAUS

All but one
Of Danaus' daughters
Made of their wedding night
A slaughter.

They butchered their husbands
In their bed,
On the very night
That they were wed.

And when each one died
She was doomed to live,
Pouring water eternally
Into a sieve.

Even the most gentle of the goddesses could be invoked to anger if given the right set of circumstances. Demeter was such a goddess. With her beautiful daughter Persephone she went about her daily business and dutifully sowed the seeds of the field and brought them to a fruitful harvest. Her life was spent quietly assisting man. On one occasion she was justifiably upset with a man named Erysichthon, who was totally given to the pleasure of food. He had little respect for god or goddess. One day he decided to build a rather extravagant banquet hall for himself. To obtain the wood necessary for the edifice he cut down the sacred grove of Demeter. Tree nymphs cried out with pain and many died from fright as he did so.

Demeter ordered him to cease. He only laughed at her. Demeter sought the assistance of the terrible goddess Famine to punish this blasphemous deed. Famine cursed Erysichthon with an insatiable appetite. Nothing could fill it. He spent his fortune in the purchase of food only to crave more of it. He even sold his daughter in an effort to obtain food to satisfy the pangs of his insatiable hunger. The poor glutton finally died from eating himself.

ERYSICHTHON

Erysichthon had an appetite,
T'was the largest one of all.
He chopped down Ceres' sacred grove
To build a banquet hall.

He didn't heed her plea to cease,
As tree nymphs died from fright.
So Famine was told to punish him
With an insatiable appetite.

He spent his fortune buying food,
Selling daughter to rebuild his wealth.
But nothing ever satisfied.
He died from eating himself.

OLYMPIAN GRATITUDE

Lest we obtain a false notion of the divine disposition in Greek Mythology we must realize that the gods were often kind to men and rewarded human goodness, favors, and worship.

We find Dionysus, the god of the vine, rewarding Midas, the mercenary king of Macedonia, for his kind protection of Silenus, the old and drunken tutor of Dionysus.

In gratitude the god promised Midas he would receive any favor he requested. The foolish Midas asked that whatever he touched would be turned into gold. As we shall see, this ill-considered request brought much trouble and grief to the foolish king.

MIDAS THE MACEDONIAN KING

When Midas saved Silenus,
The friend of wines inventor,
Bacchus owed a favor,
For Silenus was his mentor.
Promised anything he'd ask,
His request was rather bold.
He asked that everything he touched
Would immediately turn to gold.

The request was promptly granted,
But considered rather foolish.
With golden pots and pans and things,
His palace looked rather ghoulish.
When there came the dinner hour
He wondered what he'd eat.
As he began to mouth his food,
It was glittering gold, not meat.

The hunger pangs and pangs of thirst
Soon made him realize,
What he in greed had asked for
Was really not a prize.
He begged the youthful god of wine
To free him from his gold.
"Go wash in yonder river,
And you'll loose it," he was told.

So if you ever wonder where
Gold can be found today,
It's hiding in the river's sand.
It'll always be that way.

HUMANS BEWARE

The foolishness of Midas was further evidenced in another of the lovely Greek myths. Midas had been present when Marsyas challenged Apollo to the famous musical contest.

Midas, however, did not cast his vote for the divine musician. He cast his vote for Marsyas. And when one prefers a human to a god, one must pay the consequence.

The unexpected consequence is revealed in the following doggerel.

THE FOOLISH VOTE OF MIDAS

When Apollo competed
With Marsyas,
Midas thought both
Melodious.

He had listened
As they played,
But he cast his vote
The piper's way.

Apollo's pride
Was gravely dented,
When the Macedonian
King dissented.

"If your vote reflects
The way you hear,
You must be cursed
With an ass's ear."

And sure enough
When night had passed
Midas woke up
With the ears of an ass.

He grew his hair
Extremely long
To hide those ears
That had been wronged.

This is the origin
Of a saying that goes,
"Only one's hair dresser
Really knows."

OLYMPIAN RESPONSE TO PRAYER

As the Greek gods became angry, vexed, and even vengeful when offended by men, they also were most benevolent when shown the proper veneration. They not only listened to the prayers of mortals, they answered them, as we see in the story of Pygmalion, a talented young sculptor who thoroughly despised women. He was more than happy to devote himself entirely to the artistic talents with which he had been extremely endowed. He was a sculptor of great renown in work with ivory.

He once carved a statue of ivory so lovely and beautiful that he fell instantly in love with it. One day on the feast of Venus, the goddess of love, he prayed that his ivory statue would come to life. The following poem depicts the answer to his prayer.

PYGMALION

Pygmalion, male chauvinist,
The first the world had known,
Hated women with a passion
Till one of them he cloned.

He carved a maiden of ivory,
This sculptor with wonderful skill.
No woman possessed its beauty
And none there ever will.

After a time he fell in love
With this maiden he had made.
He tenderly caressed her
And dressed her in brocade.

He hung earrings on her ivory ears
And necklaces about her neck.
He even gave this counterfeit
A rather passionate peck.

Then came the feast of Venus.
All Cyprus was a fair.
Pygmalion performed her sacred rites
Then offered up a prayer.

"O god of love, I beg you
Give me for my wife
One like my ivory virgin.
Better yet, bring her to life."

Venus heard his prayerful plea,
Pygmalion went back home.
He gently kissed his statue
And found her flesh and bone.

She returned the kiss he gave
And soon the two were married.
Venus blessed their nuptials.
Over threshold bride was carried.

To this union made in heaven
There came much fame and glory.
But that's not all there is to say.
There's a moral to my story.

To rid the world of chauvinists
And make them bite the dust,
You merely need confront them
With an elephant's shapely tusk.

Another example of human prayer answered by the gods is contained in the story of Castor and Pollux. The story is rather complicated because its plot involves two sets of twins. Leda was married to Tyndareus, the king of Sparta. While Leda was carrying Tyndareus' twins within her, Zeus, disguised as a swan, appeared and loved her. Zeus also begot twins so Leda was carrying four offspring within her.

Castor and Clytemnestra, who would marry the famed Agamemnon, were the children of Tyndareus. Pollux and beautiful Helen, who would later be sought after by all men, were children of Zeus. The children of Zeus, Pollux and Helen, would be immortal. But the children of Tyndareus would die. Castor and Pollux were inseparable in life. Why should they be separated by death?

When Castor finally died, Pollux could not bear the separation. In sorrow he prayed to his father, Zeus, that a solution might be found to lessen his grief.

In answer to this prayer Zeus decreed that half of the time Castor would spend on earth with his brother Pollux. The other half Pollux would spend with Castor in Hades.

CASTOR AND POLLUX

Tyndareus was a Spartan king.
Leda was his wife.
She carried twins within her
Which she soon would bring to life.

Castor and Clytemnestra
She was about to spawn.
Then Zeus appeared and loved her,
Disguised as a big fat swan.

Where once were two, there now were four,
Adding Zeus' Pollux and Helen.
They had joined her husband's twins,
So her tummy looked like a melon.

Her boys grew up in Spartan pride,
Inseparable in every way.
Castor trained wild horses.
Pollux boxed, they say.

Castor was conceived by man
And so one day must die.
But Pollux was a son of Zeus.
Immortality was his thereby.

Castor then was struck in death,
Killed while stealing cattle.
Others say that he was killed
While in heroic battle.

Pollux asked his father, Zeus,
If immortality he could share
With his beloved brother
Whose death he couldn't bear.

Since this request was granted
They spend half their time in Hades.
The other half the inseparable twins
Walk Olympus with their ladies.

Others say the inseparable twins
Were cast into the sky.
It is there that you can see them
As Constellation Gemini.

At times mere mortals became a bother as well as a bore to the gods of Olympus and disturbed their peaceful existence. When this occurred immediate action was usually taken by the all powerful Zeus. His favorite solution to any disagreeable problem was the thunderbolt. It is depicted quite clearly in the comical story of Phaethon.

Phaethon was the son of Clymene and Helios, the god who daringly drove the Chariot of the Sun across the sky each day. One day Phaethon asked Helios to prove his fatherhood by granting him one request on the River Styx.

To his later regret Helios made such a promise. His young son foolishly asked to drive the great Chariot of the Sun across the morning sky, a foolish request indeed, but one which had to be heeded because it was sworn to on the River Styx.

The following poem reveals the chaos that followed the foolish and futile efforts of Phaethon and why Zeus was forced to act.

THE CHARIOT OF THE SUN

Phaethon, a child
Of the sun,
Thought he'd like
To have some fun.

He begged his father,
"Grant one request."
He did, not knowing
It would be grotesque.

But Helios made
A promise on Styx,
And found himself
In quite a fix.

For Phaethon's wish
Was once to drive
The Chariot of the Sun
Across the sky.

Only a god
Could hold those steeds
From accomplishing
Their tragic deeds.

But a promise made
Meant a promise kept,
Even though Phaethon
Was most inept.

He led the sun
Too close to Utopia,
Which now is known
As Ethiopia.

Too close to the mountains,
Never seeing,
Volcanoes suddenly
Came into being.

Helpless earth
Cried out to Zeus,
And he a lightning
Bolt let loose.

This was the end
Of rash young Phaethon.
He fell to the earth
Like well-fried bacon.

Almighty Zeus heard and answered the prayers of people and the pleas and petitions of the lesser gods, but only as their prayer was worded, not as it should have been worded or as the petitioner intended to word it.

Sometimes this proved to be quite awkward. Such was the case in the prayer of Aurora. Aurora was the goddess of Dawn. She fell in love with a mortal by the name of Tithonius, the son of Laomedon and the brother of King Priam.

Aurora prayed that her young lover would never die. Zeus faithfully answered her prayer, but only as her prayer was stated. In her prayerful request the unfortunate Aurora had foolishly forgotten to ask for perpetual youth.

As time passed and years followed years Tithonius grew older and older. His bones rattled noisily as he hobbled along. He was old and tired and feeble.

The following poem explains how the dilemma of eternal aging was solved.

THE ORIGIN OF THE FROG

Tithonius was
A handsome lad
Whom Aurora took
To share her pad.

She prayed that he
Would never die.
And on the gods
She could rely.

But in her prayer
She really goofed.
She forgot to ask
For eternal youth.

Decrepitude with time
He logged.
Aurora turned him
Into a frog.

OLYMPIAN RETRIBUTION

The gods were so clever in their dealings with mortals that at times they punished man without man even knowing it. The case of Pandora, a gift from the gods to man, was just such a punishment.

After the Titan War and after the great monsters that roamed the earth had been destroyed, the Titan Prometheus now thought the world safe enough for man. He created man to cause problems and much difficulty for the Olympian gods.

Prometheus wondered what singular gift he could give his new creation. His brother, Epimetheus, had created the animals, and in so doing he had exhausted the more common gifts. Their sight, their speed, their senses and hunting skills were far superior to anything he could give man.

He then thought of the gift of fire. By its possession man would be above all other creatures. Prometheus, then stole a fiery flame from the heavens and gave it as a gift to man.

Needless to say, the gods were angered at the impudent theft. They decided to create woman in order to punish man. The craftsman Hephaetus was commissioned to form her. He exceeded even his own ingenuity in performing the task. Each of the goddesses was called upon to present Pandora with a special gift. Hermes was sent to present her to Prometheus. But he was far too wise to accept any gift that gods would bestow. Epimetheus, however, was quick to accept her for his wife in spite of the warnings of his more experienced brother.

The beautiful and exciting Pandora came bearing a little box. It had been filled many years before by evil goddesses Night and Eris.

PANDORA

When fire was taken from heaven
It created quite a fuss.
It was given as a gift to man
By the Titan Prometheus.

He created man to cause the gods
A little bit of trouble.
But gods, of course, won't be outdone.
They would cause man trouble double.

Prometheus warned his brother:
"Refuse gifts that gods bestow."
He'd learned the bitter lesson,
That they only bring one woe.

Epimetheus was rather foolish,
Not prone to take advice.
When Pandora came with her little box,
He took her as his wife.

The little box she opened,
And out jumped ominous things,
Envy, hate and jealousy,
And everything evil brings.

She quickly closed the cover,
This silly little dope.
She saved one thing from fleeing.
It was the gift of hope.

FATE

The Fates were the terrible daughters of Night. They were assigned to determine the destinies of men. As men were born their very span of life was determined by the Fates.

These Fates were three in number, Clotho, Lachesis, and Atropos. Clotho spins the thread of life. It is then measured by Lachesis and snipped by Atropos. Thus is man's span of life determined. He is powerless in the face of the Fates. Determinism is the law of life.

The stories of Meleager and Polycrates center on decrees of Fate. The poems are self-explanatory.

THE CALYDONIAN BOAR HUNT

The threads of Fate
Are sometimes worn,
Even on the
Day we're born.

This was the case
With Meleager,
Who soon in infant death
Would swagger.

"When burning log
Will lie in coal,
His span of life
Will reach its goal."

So mother snatched
The log away,
Meleager saw
Another day.

He grew in age
And in hunting skilled,
And reached renown
By the boar he killed.

The head he gave
To fair Atlanta.
But his uncles despised
His playing Santa.

"Such a trophy
Should belong to men
Giving to a girl,
The unforgivable sin."

They persisted in carping
About the head.
Their nephew in rage
Then struck them dead.

The headless boar
And two cadavers,
Were carried home
By Meleager.

When Althea saw
The parricide
The long hid log
She could no longer hide.

She placed it on
The blazing fire,
And Meleager
Soon expired.

THE RING OF POLYCRATES

There was a king
With a precious ring,
Polycrates, all men called him.
And to this name
There came great fame
As wealth and riches sought him.

Then warned by friends
Fate makes amends,
Good fortune can't always be.
Not to be a fool
He took his jewel
And cast it into the sea.

Perhaps this would rate,
Delay of Fate
And he could go on living.
But that night he ate
A fish just baked,
And found ring with much misgiving.

When dawn appeared
He froze with fear.
Fate had won, he realized.
Now he must go
To King Pluto
Fortune was equalized.

Even brave men feared the Fates and trembled as they approached. Only the undaunted Heracles ever defied them. This defiance of Fate is told in the beautiful love story of Admetis and Alcestis.

The Fates had informed King Admetis that he must die unless he could find someone who was willing to take his place in Hades, the realm of the dead.

Admetis begged his servants and his friends. They emphatically declined his invitation. He pleaded with his aged parents. They too refused to take his place in death.

When all seemed lost, his loving wife stepped forward. Alcestis was readily willing to lay down her own life for her husband.

In the hour of her death Heracles came by and discovered the painful tragedy the household awaited in grief. The awesome and bold giant placed himself at the door of the castle, wrestled with Lord Death, and made him return Alcestis to health.

Heracles defeated the Fates, a deed which not even gods can do.

ADMETIS AND ALCESTIS

Admetus, king of Pherae
Was told by Fate he'd die,
Unless he found a sucker
Who in his place would lie.

He asked both friend and servant
To take his place in death.
But they refused to play his game,
They were too fond of breath.

He begged his aged parents
Who had little left of life.
They, too, refused his offer.
There was only left his wife.

Alcestis was most willing
To suffer in his stead.
Her love was sacrificial
From the day that they were wed.

Just before Lord Death arrived
Heracles paid a call.
When he heard about the tragic news,
He stood up ten feet tall.

When the knock of death was sounded,
Heracles opened the gate.
With all his mighty firmness
He told death he'd have to wait.

Thus king and queen lived many years.
Admetis revered his wife.
Would there be such a one today
Who would offer up her life.

GREEK HEROES

The same Heracles who had defeated the Fates was the greatest of the many Greek Heroes. He was a son of Zeus and Alcmene. Although married to modest Megara, he had many love affairs.

He was the strongest man on earth, dear to the Olympians for he had assisted them in defeating the giants who sought to overthrow Olympus. He was as dull-witted as he was strong and prone to fits of anger which often resulted in needless slaughter.

He was born in Thebes. Iphicles was his twin brother, although Iphicles, so dear to Heracles, was begotten by a human father, Amphitryon. Hera, always jealous of bastard offspring of Zeus, sent serpents to destroy him in his cradle. The infant Heracles strangled them without difficulty.

At eighteen he set out on great exploits to rid the world of monsters and wild beasts. He had three sons by Megara, but went insane and killed his sons and their mother. He was purified in Athens and told by the oracle to enroll in the service of his cousin, Eurystheus, who then assigned him twelve impossible tasks to perform. Many tales surrounding this hero concern these labors.

He now married Deianira. As he was crossing a river taking her home the rascally Centaur, Nessus, acted as a ferryman. The Centaur ran off with the bride. Heracles shot him with an arrow dipped in the very venomous blood of the Hydra, the frightful offspring of Typhon and Echidna.

Dying, the Centaur pretended to be remorseful and told Deianira that she should take some of his blood and use it as a charm to win back Heracles if he were ever unfaithful. When she later learned of his affair with Iole, she dipped his robe in the blood and sent it to her husband, hoping to win back his love.

When Heracles put on the robe he felt the fire of the Hydra's venom flow through his veins. In pain he returned home to die. When the unsuspecting Deianira realized her crime, she took her own life.

Heracles built a funeral pyre and climbed upon it. The fire was lit. Lightning struck and the dead hero achieved immortality and ascended to Olympus. He married Hebe, the daughter of Zeus and Hera, and now lives with the gods.

HERACLES

Heracles did heroic deeds,
This bastard child of Zeus.
Juno always bugged him,
From this life to set him loose.

Serpents he killed in the cradle,
Lions and dragon when a man.
He traveled over all the earth,
Driving bandits and beasts from the land.

For Eurytheus twelve years he labored,
Accomplishing unbelievable feats.
Prometheus he saved from the eagle,
And his liver on which it feasts.

A girdle he stole from Hippolyte,
And angered the Amazon.
From monsters he saved Hesione,
The daughter of Laomedon.

He killed the Centaur, Nessus,
Who stole Deianira and galloped off.
Because of this he died one day.
And in death did Nessus scoff.

Now he lives on Olympus,
The porter of gods so great.
Hebe, Juno's messenger,
Is his eternal mate.

Theseus was another of the truly great Greek heroes, brave like Heracles, but far more compassionate and infinitely more intelligent. He was the son of Aegeus, the king of Athens. His mother was Aethra, whom Aegeus abandoned.

When Aegeus abandoned his wife and son he buried a sword beneath a rock and told Aethra that when Theseus grew and was strong enough to lift the rock, he was to pick up the sword and come to Athens.

Theseus grew into manhood, strong beyond all others. His mother then told him the story of the sword. Immediately he set out for Athens on foot, seeking to imitate Heracles, his hero, as he journeyed along.

When he arrived in Athens the witch Medea, now the wife of Aegeus, knew who he was and sought to poison him. At that very instant Aegeus recognized the sword and spilled the poisoned cup. The witch Medea fled to Asia where she founded the Medes.

Every seven years Athens was required to send seven youth and seven maidens to Crete to serve as food for the monster Minotaur. This served as atonement for the death of King Minos' son who had been killed by a wild bull when sent by the king of Athens to slay it.

The Minotaur was half bull and half human. It was the offspring of Minos' wife Pasiphae and a beautiful white bull that Poseidon made her fall madly in love with to punish Minos.

When Pasiphae gave birth to this monster bull, Minos ordered Daedalus to make an inescapable labyrinth to house it. It was fed with hostages sent from Athens every seven years.

While Athens was mourning the hostages departed for Crete. Theseus, disguised as a hostage, set sail with them. He vowed to destroy the disgusting monster. The hostage ship always sailed under it's black sails. Theseus told his father the ship would return to Athens under white sails if the mission were successful and he were safe.

When the hostages arrived in Crete, Ariadne, the daughter of Minos, fell in love with the Athenian hero, promising to help him if he would make her his bride. She then obtained a magic string from Daedalus to assist Theseus in the maze. With the promised help Theseus entered the labyrinth, killed the Minotaur with his own hands, escaped by the magic string, and fled with Ariadne. He abandoned her on the Island of Naxos where Bacchus took her as his wife.

In the chaos of the events which followed, Theseus forgot to change the sails. When his father saw the black sails on the distant horizon, he jumped from his castle tower into the sea, which has ever since been called by his name, Aegean.

Theseus succeeded his father as king of Athens. Under his leadership the city grew and greatly prospered.

A CRETAN BULL STORY

Pasiphae made love
With a Cretan bull,
And soon with child
She was full.

And when at last
There came her hour,
She begot
The minotaur.

"What'll I do
With that dog-gone cow?"
Minos said to his court
With wrinkled brow.

"My castle is
Already full.
There's hardly room
For this monstrous bull."

"I know," he said
In a sudden daze,
"I'll have Daedalus make him
A lovely maze.

It can eat my enemy,
The Athenian Greek,
If he loses my maze game
Of hide and seek."

But Theseus, our hero,
Appeared on the isle,
And killed off the bull
In heroic style.

He solved the maze
With a magic string,
A gift from Ariadne,
Fair child of the king.

He took Ariadne
To be his wife,
Setting out for home
In flight for his life.

But Bacchus already
Had staked her in claim.
So Theseus abandoned
This gorgeous dame.

The silly guy
Forgot the sail.
The black one made
Aegeus wail.

He jumped into
The sea insane.
The sea now bears
His funny name.

When Theseus journeyed to Athens as a young man, he met all kinds of strange people on the way. One of the strangest was Sinis, the Pinebinder, so called because in his perversity he tied people to pines that he had bent over and tied to the ground. Then he cut the rope and watched them fly.

Even more strange was Procrustes, the father of Sinis. He was a real sickie. He was overjoyed to welcome overnight guests. Each had to fit his beds. He had a short bed for tall people and long bed for short people. Those who were short he stretched on a rack until they fit and those who were tall he chopped up a little at a time until they fit.

SINIS THE PINEBINDER

Sinis, the Pinebinder,
Was quite a guy
Tying men to bent pines,
He let them fly.

This was routine,
Till Theseus passed by.
Now you'll find Sinis,
Somewhere in the sky.

INHOSPITABLE HOSPITALITY

Procrustes was hospitable,
Until his guests came in.
He played with them a little game,
And it surely wasn't gin.

He had two beds within his house,
One short, the other long.
He matched his guests unto the beds,
But he always did it wrong.

The short were put in longest bed,
The big were put in small.
The tall were cut until they fit,
And short were stretched till tall.

PERITHOUS AND THESEUS

Perithous and Theseus
Had an altercation,
But it was settle peacefully
By mutual admiration.

Each pledged the other friendship.
This pledge was made for life.
And just about this very time,
Each did lose his wife.

Freed, they thought to have some fun
And steal a real beauty.
No one less than Helen
Would they accept as booty.

They came to Sparta and stole her
And cast lots for whose she'd be.
Theseus was the winner.
It was the Fates' decree.

Perithous sought to sooth himself
By abducting Hades' Queen.
He journeyed to the Netherworld
And since has not been seen.

Theseus accompanied him
To lend a helping hand
In abducting Queen Persephone
From her wonder underland.

King Pluto caught them in their deed
And sentenced them to Hades.
This would be their punishment
For chasing after ladies.

Great Heracles saved Theseus
From Pluto's dark decree.
He took him back up to the earth
So daylight he could see.

While Theseus was a prisoner
For his lecherous deed,
Helen's brothers free her
And his kingdom went to seed.

Rebellion soon dethroned him.
He fled to his estate.
Lycomedes pushed him off a cliff
And he became shark bait.

The moral of this story
Is all there's left to tell.
To get a lovely lady
Never go to hell.

MYTHOLOGICAL BIRDS

When King Minos discovered that Theseus had penetrated the maze, killed the Minotaur, and fled with his daughter, he knew that he could not have done so without the artful assistance of Daedalus, its ingenious inventor. He threw Daedalus and his son, Icarus, into prison.

There Daedalus made two pairs of wings of wax and feathers to flee the island. He warned Icarus not to fly too high lest the sun melt the wax. As they flew from Crete, the wonder of new power went to the boy's head and he flew ever upward, paying no heed to his father's shouts of warning. The sun melted the wax and Icarus fell into the sea and drowned.

Daedalus stopped to bury his son and named the land after him. He then went on to Sicily where he became the tutor of his nephew, Perdix. The lad learned well and soon surpassed his tutor. It was Perdix who invented the saw and the compass.

Daedalus in a fit of envy threw his nephew from a tower. Before he crashed to the earth Athena, the goddess of wisdom, who valued invention, turned Perdix into a partridge, a bird that still has a fear of heights and so makes its nest in bushes.

DAEDALUS AND ICARUS

The labyrinth failed,
Its inventor was jailed,
King Minos was quite upset.
The kingdom of Crete
Is an island seat,
To escape one must get wet.

The king guards the land,
And even sea sand,
But he does not rule the sky.
If Daedalus will flee,
Minoan tyranny,
It's this way he must try.

So Daedalus tries
To conquer the skies
With wings that he invented.
With feathers and wax
And guards grown lax,
The island was absented.

Son, Icarus, too,
With Daedalus fled
With minimal instruction.
"Do not fly too low."
Was the wise bon-mot,
"Water means destruction."

"And, son, please do not soar,
Toward the sun's corridor,
Its heat will melt your wax.
Just stay near me,
And we'll soon be free,
The Fates we must not tax."

So off they went,
Toward Sicily bent.
As ploughman stopped to gaze.
The hyena laughed,
Shepherds leaned on staff,
To view the maker of maze.

Icarus exulted,
Heavenward he vaulted,
Too close to the sun he came.
Within the sun's ring,
The fragile wing
Was melted by its flame.

Like a falling star,
He tumbled far,
And rested in the water,
When the deed was done,
Father held his son,
And sang a Stabat Pater.

He placed in earth,
This child of birth,
A tombstone marks the area.
And before he left,
With grief bereft,
He named the land Icaria.

Daedalus became
With envy insane
When called to tutor Perdix.
This inventive lad
Drove Daedalus mad
Their genius didn't at all mix.

From tower is thrown
A youth not yet grown.
By an uncle very mean.
But ere he hit the ground
With a crashing sound,
He was partridged by Athene.

So partridges won't be
In high nest or tree,
Nor in any place that's tall.
For when it is high,
Far up in the sky,
It is mindful of it's fall.

As Athena changed Perdix into a partridge to save him from death, so also did other gods turn other people into birds when by their behavior they proved a problem to the gods. We see this in the myth of Procne and Philomela, perhaps the most gruesome of all Greek myths.

Tereus, the king of Thrace, made a journey to Athens to ask King Pandion for the lovely hand of his oldest daughter, Procne. They returned to Thrace and were soon married. They had a charming son name Itys. After five years of marriage Procne sorely missed her younger sister, Philomela. To sooth his wife's anxiety, Tereus consented to return to her father's house to bring Philomela back for a visit. Procne was overjoyed and Tereus departed.

Philomela had grown into a very beautiful young woman. When Tereus saw her, he was filled with lust. Upon their arrival in Thrace the King took her to his hunting lodge and raped her. He then cut out her tongue lest she reveal the crime. He chained her in the lodge where he left a maid servant to tend her.

Tereus told Procne that her sister had died on the journey. She mourned bitterly.

Although Philomela could not speak with words, she spoke eloquently in her weaving and revealed every sordid detail in the tapestry she wove. The maid servant was asked to bring the tapestry to the queen as a gift.

As soon as Procne saw it she realized the whole truth. She followed the servant and released her dear sister. In tears they returned to the castle to devise a punishment for the king befitting his crime. Procne chopped up little Itys, made him into a stew and fed him to his father.

When Tereus came to know the truth he pursued in anger the sisters now leaving the castle. As he was about to catch Procne and Philomela the Fates turned him into a crow. They turned Philomela into a swallow, a bird that cannot sing. And Procne became the mournful nightingale, mourning that she had killed her son.

CROWS-NIGHTINGALES-SWALLOWS

Tereus, the Thracian king,
Went to a foreign land.
He asked the king of Athens
For his lovely daughter's hand.

So Procne married Tereus,
And thus became the queen.
But she missed her little sister,
Whom five years she hadn't seen.

So off again for Athens,
Tereus for Philomela.
Wow! Had she matured
In the eyes of this lusty fella.

They crossed the sea and came to Thrace,
Sister-in-law and king.
And who is there who would ever think
He'd do an incestuous thing.

No sooner had they landed
Than Tereus pulled a caper.
Taking Philomela to his lodge,
It was there that he did rape her.

Such a terrible thing as this,
Must always be unsung.
So he chained her to the lodge's wall
And then cut out her tongue.

A maid was left to tend her.
To castle he came quite bold.
To trusting wife, dear Procne,
And son, Itys, five years old.

Procne went in mourning,
Told sister died on ship.
For it was her love of Procne
That had brought her on this trip.

Back to Philomela,
Now tongueless in her jail.
Her hatred found an ingenious way,
To speak a kind of braille.

She wove the entire story,
Every sordid little scene.
And her naive little servant
Took tapestry to the queen.

When Procne saw the weaving,
The awful truth was known.
She wished she had Medusa's head
To turn Tereus into stone.

She followed the little servant.
Philomela she embraced.
She then devised a punishment
Befitting the disgrace.

She chopped up little Itys
And made the king a stew.
But when the king discovered
From the castle sisters flew.

Tereus pursued in chase,
But justice the Fates bestow.
When just about to catch and kill,
They turned king into a crow.

The sisters still are seen in flight,
Procne, a nightingale,
Chirping out her doleful tunes,
Over killing first-born male.

Philomela is a swallow,
Victim of the king.
She only tweets and twitters,
With a tongue that cannot sing.

Many of today's birds once walked the earth as proud Greeks until angry gods changed them into feathered, flying creatures. This is what happened in the story of Scylla.

The powerful Minos made war upon the little kingdom of Megara. For some strange reason he simply couldn't conquer it. The reason was a decree of Fate. The Fates had decided that nothing could destroy little Magara as long as its king, Nisus, wore a purple lock of hair.

As King Minos paraded outside the city gates, Syclla, the daughter of King Nisus, fell madly in love with him. One night she cut off the purple lock from her father's hair, took it to Minos, and explained to him why he had not been victorious.

Minos loathed the girl for her betrayal of both father and country. He cursed the traitor, abandoned the war, and set sail for Crete. Scylla, in her insane love, jumped into the sea and attached herself to the ship's rudder.

At that moment the gods turned her into a sea bird and her father into a great eagle that swooped down and devoured her.

A DAUGHTER'S BETRAYAL

Megara's king was Nisus,
And Scylla was his daughter.
Minos was the king of Crete,
Who came warring cross the water.

Six months the siege had lasted,
Megara still was strong.
Crete was far superior,
So something must be wrong.

The reason was a decree of Fate,
That Megara would stand like rock.
No enemy could conquer her.
While king's hair had purple lock.

Minos arrayed in armor,
Won Scylla's admiration.
This silly girl then fell in love
And acted in desperation.

She plotted against her father,
And filial love did mock.
As Nisus lay in bed asleep.
She cut off the fatal lock.

She fled into the enemy camp,
Demanding to see the king.
She presented him the purple lock,
And also her heart string.

Minos abhorred her filial cunning.
He cursed the love sick girl,
Who betrayed both father and fatherland,
And the flag of treason unfurled.

He came to terms with Nisus.
Cursing Scylla he sailed for home.
Silly Scylla, love sick traitor,
Jumped into the sea of foam.

She seized the great ship's rudder,
Shouting out her love.
The gods made Nisus an eagle,
That soars the sky above.

He pounced upon his daughter,
Striking with claw and beak.
She had now become a sea bird,
Which eagles love to seek.

Today we still see eagles
Into heavens climb,
Then dive and kill these sea birds,
Vengeance for an ancient crime.

The tale of the crow is another interesting story about birds in Greek Mythology. There was a time when crows were a very beautiful white. The change of color was a punishment of Apollo.

There lived in Thessaly a beautiful young girl name Coronis. Apollo saw her, loved her, and took her to be his wife. Soon she carried his child, Asclepius, who would later bring much renown to the healing arts.

The foolish Coronis, however, preferred a human love to the love of a god. She had a love affair with Ischys, hoping that she might conceal it from Apollo. But Apollo had never really trusted his new bride and had left his favorite bird, the beautiful white crow, to watch over her and protect his interests in his absence.

When the white crow witnessed the shocking conduct of Coronis, it flew off to inform its master. Apollo became quite angry with the faithful bird for not plucking out the eyes of Ischys. In his anger he changed the crows color to a very dirty black.

Apollo called upon his sister, Artemis, to shoot the unfaithful Coronis with an unerring arrow. When Coronis was placed upon the funeral pyre, Apollo recalled that she was with child. The child was cut out by Hermes, placed in the care of the Centaur Cheiron, and taught the art of healing.

WHY CROWS CHANGED COLOR

There was a time when crows were white.
They made a rather pretty sight.
Now they're black, of course, you know.
The change occurred quite long ago.

The story is extremely strange,
That gives the reason for the change.
The crow was once Apollo's friend.
And that is where we must begin.

The trusted crow chaperoned his love,
Apollo gone, crow watched above.
It flew up high, but watched the ground,
Lest Apollo's love would horse around.

But Coronis was a little wild,
Even while carrying Apollo's child.
She should have cleaned or washed the dishes,
But instead she had an affair with Ischys.

So off to Apollo sped the bird
Telling all it saw and all it heard.
Apollo cursed his feathered spy
That should have plucked out Ischys' eye.

The friendship with Apollo became estranged
And this is when crow's color changed.
It didn't do what he thought it could,
And what it could have done, he thought it should.

The crow was victim of Apollo's flack
And became a very dirty black.
Unfaithful Coronis was sentenced to pyre
Apollo thought of his child when seeing the fire.

This son of Apollo was unbeguiled
So Hermes was sent to cut out the child.
Asclepius was saved while the pyre was burning
And sent off to Chiron for scholarly learning.

He became the father of healing arts,
And could bring back life once it departs.
The gods became angry at skills so abstruse,
So the clever Asclepius was zapped by Zeus.

So learn the lesson that black crows tell
And all in life will go very well.
We should have done what we could,
For what we can do, we always should.

THE ARGONAUTS

Perhaps the most interesting of all heroic journeys in Greek Mythology is the journey of Jason in quest of the golden fleece. It was a journey by water. There were no roads. Seas and rivers were the only highways, and they were uncharted. Sailors had to put to shore each night and strange shores found monsters and giants in waiting.

The story begins with Athamas, a Greek king who tired of his wife, Nephele, and married Ino, a daughter of Cadmus. Nephele feared for the life of her two children, Helle and Phrixus. Their step-mother would surely kill them so that her own children could inherit the kingdom.

Nephele prayed to the gods and Hermes was sent with a golden ram that flew off with the children. As the ram flew over the sea, Helle fell off and drowned. This strait now bears her name, Hellespont. Phrixus was brought safely to land in the county of Colchis. There he sacrificed the ram to Zeus and gave its golden fleece to Aetes, king of Colchis.

HELLE AND PHRIXUS

Helle and Phrixus
Were sister and brother,
Not at all liked
By their new step-mother.

So fearful father
Told them to scram,
And sent them off
On a golden ram.

Helle fell off
In her efforts to flee.
There's a place called Hellespont
Now known in that sea.

Jason was a cousin of Phrixus and the rightful heir to his father's throne. The throne had been usurped by Jason's uncle, the deceitful Pelias. When the young Jason appeared to claim his kingdom, his uncle informed him that he must first bring back the famed golden fleece.

The proposed adventure delighted the daring youth. He called upon all the heroes of Greece to accompany him in his quest for the golden fleece. All the great heroes assembled: Heracles, Orpheus, Castor and Pollux and many more. Jason led the expedition. They set sail in a ship called the Argo. They were called Argonauts.

Their journey was a pilgrimage of peril, and their conquests would be told by Greeks for years to come. No one questioned their bravery, but it was only by the help of the prophetic powers of the blinded seer Phineus, whom they assisted by driving off the Harpies, that they were able to succeed and arrive at their destination.

The story of Phineus and his problems makes for interesting reading.

PHINEUS AND THE HARPIES

Phineus was an unfortunate man,
Once the king of Thrace.
Apollo blessed him with prophesy,
The future he could trace.

But Phineus angered Olympian gods
By committing a terrible crime.
He allowed his second wife
To make his children blind.

Such a deed enraged the gods,
Who closely watch mankind.
So avenging Zeus gave king a choice,
Tween death and going blind.

His choice was total darkness,
Till the end of life.
This enraged the sun god,
Who brought him further strife.

Angered Helios then sent Harpies,
Each an ugly bird-like wench,
To torment the blinded Phineus
With their very loathsome stench.

They befouled the food he tried to eat
And then they flew away.
The poor old guy was starving,
Nearer death each single day.

Then the Argonauts happened by
And saw the blind man's plight.
Calais and Zetes, sons of the Wind,
Pursued the Harpies in their flight.

They were about to kill them
When Iris did appear.
The Rainbow Messenger of the gods
Made her message very clear.

They must not harm the Harpies,
This Father Zeus decreed.
They would cease afflicting Phineus,
In punishment for his deed.

The weakened, blinded victim,
Now could eat his food.
Directing Argonauts to Colchis,
To show his gratitude.

With this help from blinded seer,
The Argonauts departed.
They succeeded in their mission,
Only cause they were kind-hearted.

The Argonauts finally arrived at Colchis. The gods were watching over them in the dangers that they faced. Hera, herself, was their protectress. She enlisted the aid of Aphrodite's son Cupid who made the daughter of the king of Colchis fall in love with Jason. Her name was Medea, a witch with magical powers. She is found time and time again in Greek Mythology.

When the king discovered why they had come, he was angry and plotted their death by demanding impossible feats for them to perform before he would grant them the golden fleece. They performed these deeds through the aid of Medea and her magical powers.

Medea then informed Jason that the king was about to kill them and he must steal the fleece on that very night. She would help him kill the dragon that guarded it, if he would take her as his wife.

The fleece was stolen and the Argonauts set sail for home with Medea and her younger brother, a lad named Absyrtus. King Aetes followed in angry pursuit. When about to overtake the Argonauts, Medea chopped up her brother and threw the pieces into the sea. Aetes stopped to pick up those pieces and the Argonauts escaped.

POOR LITTLE ABSYRTUS

Jason stole
The golden fleece,
Aided by Medea,
Circe's niece.

She was a witch
With foreboding power,
And concoctions she mixed
In the castle tower.

She exchanged her brews
For the love of Jason,
And from Aetes' army
They quickly hastened.

To slow down her father
Who was pursuing,
A dastardly plan
In her head was a brewing.

Half brother Absyrtus,
She cut into pieces
As they sped to Ioclus
With the golden fleeces.

The father stopped
To gather his son,
So Jason and Medea
Their freedom won.

A LOVE STORY

As Greek Mythology contains tales of heroic battles, journeys, and conquests, so too does it contain marvelous stories of love. One of the most beautiful stories in all Greek Mythology is the story of Psyche and Cupid, the god of love.

There once was a king who fathered three daughters. All were lovely, but the youngest was so beautiful that suitors were truly afraid to approach her. Her two sisters had long been married, but no one asked for Psyche's hand. Saddened, she consulted an oracle who told her to go to a mountain top and there she would find her true love.

She did as she was told and on the mountain top she heard a voice that told her to go to a nearby castle. There her lover would come to her each night, but she must never, never look at him.

In the following bit of doggerel the plot is unfolded.

PYSCHE AND CUPID

Pysche, fair maid of royalty,
Was the prettiest child of three.
Two had wed, but not the third,
Her beauty made suitors flee.

She called upon an oracle,
To find out what to do.
"Go to far off mountain top.
There your lover waits for you."

Said gentle voice from mountain top,
"Go to the castle you see.
I'll come to you each single night,
But never look at me."

Happiness embraced her life,
As oracle did decree.
She loved her lover very much,
But never did him see.

When sisters paid her visit,
They soon did disagree.
They said about her lover,
"A dragon he must be."

They told her she must peak that night,
And gave her torch and knife.
And if he be a monster,
She must take his life.

She followed orders given her,
It was really very stupid.
For when she looked, what did she see?
It was the love god Cupid.

He woke right up and stalked away,
Not accepting her contrition.
For as a god, he knew so well,
Love cannot survive suspicion.

A TRAGEDY

Some myths are tales of beautiful sacrificial love while the others are tales of tragedy. Lives were lived under the cruel domination of the Fates. The tragic tale of Oedipus depicts this domination.

Laius was the king of Thebes. His wife was Jocasta. The oracle of Delphi had informed Laius that he would die at the hand of his own son. When a son was born to Laius, mindful of the prophesy, he pierced the child's feet (Oedipus means swollen feet) and placed him on the top of a mountain to die.

Shepherds found the abandoned child and took him to the childless king and queen of Corinth, Polybus and Merope, who lovingly raised him.

Oedipus was later told by the same Oracle that he would kill his father and marry his mother, whom he thought were Polybus and Merope. Horrified at such a prospect, the young Oedipus fled his homeland and set out for Thebes. On the way a stranger insulted him. In the scuffle that followed Oedipus killed the stranger. It was Laius.

Approaching Thebes Oedipus soon confronted the Sphinx, a giant monster that paralyzed the country side by devouring all who could not answer the riddle it asked. "What is it that walks on four feet in the morning, two feet at noon, and three feet at night?" When Oedipus answered, "Man", the Sphinx was so embarrassed by the ease with which he answered that she immediately killed herself.

Oedipus was proclaimed hero and king. He married Queen Jocasta, the widow of Laius and his own mother. He knew neither fact at this time.

Many years later when the blinded seer Teiresias finally revealed the awful truth, Jocasta killed herself, Oedipus blinded himself and went into exile with his faithful daughter and companion, Antigone.

OEDIPUS REX

When Oracle said,
He'd kill his father one day,
Laius sent
Young Oedipus away.

Reared by Polybus
Whom he thought was his sire,
He fled quickly from home,
Lest Polybus expire.

While traveling afar,
And insulted on path,
He gave stranger Laius
A sudden blood bath.

He solved the riddle
Of the famous Sphinx,
And celebrated
With spirituous drinks.

The people immediately
Made him their king,
And decked him out
With crown and ring.

Jocasta, his mother,
Became his wife.
He was doomed to live
A cursed life.

His children were really
His sisters and brothers.
Now came the time
That he discovers.

He plucked out his eyes
In deep remorse,
And roamed the earth
On a stupid horse.

Faithful Antigone
Stayed by his side.
The earth swallowed him up.
That's how he died.

THE TROJAN WAR

Perhaps the most interesting event in mythological history is the famed Trojan War fought between Sparta and Troy. After Paris, the son of King Priam of Troy, stole Helen, the wife of Menelaus, the king of Sparta, the Spartans set out in bloody battle to win back their queen.

Since the Greeks in some way attributed all things to their gods, it is to be expected that the gods would play an important part in the great conflict.

Ultimately the war was caused by Eris, the goddess of Strife and Discord. She was the sister of Ares, the god of War. This troublesome goddess was not invited to the wedding of Peleus and Thetis. She caused too much of a problem by her presence. Snubbed, she sought revenge by throwing a golden apple marked "For the fairest" into the gathering. Three goddesses made claim that it was meant for them: Venus, Hera, and Athena. Zeus was asked to settle the argument, but in his wisdom he declined the invitation and appointed Paris, the young shepherd son of King Priam, to determine the rightful claimant.

Each goddess offered Paris a bribe. Hera offered power. Athena offered wisdom. Aprhodite offered Paris the most beautiful woman in the world. Needless to say, Paris accepted the offer of Aphrodite. Helen was to be his wife. The Trojan War was about to begin.

THE APPLE OF DISCORD

It wasn't cause
Her breath was bad,
That invitations to Eris
Were forbade.
Nor was it her manners
All abhorred,
That the Goddess of Strife
Was so ignored.

Her very presence
Said: "Beware.
I've a disposition
Like a bear."
From Olympic weddings
She was excluded.
Her pent up anger
Now exuded.

If gods would keep her
Safe afar,
She would start
The Trojan War.
She threw into
The nuptial party
A golden apple
Hale and hearty.

For the fairest,
It was signed.
Perhaps, it was
Even underlined.
Three laid claim
It was meant for them,
Juno, Athene, and Venus,
Victims of Eris' whim.

Zeus was sought
For the judge's role.
He wouldn't touch it
With a ten foot pole.
He decreed: "Paris,
Priam's shepherd son,
He will judge
To see who's won."

All three goddesses
Offered bribes,
Power, victory,
Or the prettiest bride.
The offer of Venus
Was accepted by Paris.
And Helen was his,
If steal her he darest.

He left Oenome
And set out from Troy.
To Sparta he journeyed
For Venus' ploy.
He spent some days
In the royal house,
And stole the wife
Of Menelaus.

The abduction discovered
Upon their departure,
Spartans assembled
Both swordsman and archers.
They set sail for Troy
To win back their queen.
It was a rather
Bloody scene.

History calls it
The Trojan War.
The Trojans appeared
The inferior.
This means they lost
The war, of course,
It had something to do
With a hobby horse.

As the gods played an important part in the cause of the Trojan War, so also did they exercise an influence in the many phases and aspects of it. Hardly had the Greeks assembled the ships at Aulis to set sail for Troy, than we see the intervention of the goddess Artemis.

Agamemnon, the brother of Menelaus, was in charge of the great army of Greek heroes and soldiers whose services had been enlisted. All were ready and eager to embark upon their journey to Troy. But the winds were not favorable and they were forced to remain in port.

The seer Calchas then informed them that this was a punishment of the goddess Artemis whom Agamemnon had recently offended. Until the required sacrificial atonement was duly offered, the army of Greeks would be unable to depart.

Calchas then informed the arrogant Agamemnon that the victim of this sacrifice must be none other than his own daughter, Iphigeneia. For the honor of Greece Agamemnon at last consented in sadness to the demands of the goddess. He sent for Iphigeneia under the pretext that she was to marry Achilles.

The victim was offered in sacrifice. Artemis was placated. The winds became favorable and the Greeks sailed for Troy.

IPHIGENIA

The fleet was now assembled,
About to sail for Troy.
Agamemnon offended Diana,
And she was quite annoyed.

Vexed by his irreverent act,
The goddess calmed the wind.
Until came needed sacrifice,
It would never blow again.

Ships idled on the waters,
Waiting for the wind.
Calchas then informed them,
They must first atone for sin.

The king's daughter, Iphigenia,
Must be offered in sacrifice.
There was no doubt about it.
The instructions were precise.

Agamemnon then in sorrow,
Gave up his high command.
But Menelaus convinced him
He must meet the god's demand.

So father sent for daughter,
To wed Achilles was the guise.
But the plot was soon discovered,
And the evil of fatherly lies.

Iphigenia with matchless courage,
Sacrificed her life.
She bared her throat unto the blade,
Falling victim to the knife.

Then the winds began to blow
And men went down to ships.
They embarked upon the Trojan War
With brave maiden's name on lips.

At last the Greeks arrived at Troy. They were reluctant to leave their ships for an oracle had informed them that the first to set foot on enemy soil would die. Protesilaus then demonstrated heroic courage and went ashore. He killed several Trojans, but then was soon slaughtered.

For nine long years there were skirmishes, but little progress was made. A duel between Paris and Menelaus was a draw. Hector and Ajax also fought to a draw. Famous Achilles, pouting over a disappointment in love, withdrew from battle. It was only after Hector had slain his companion, Patroclus, that Achilles again entered the foray and killed Hector. Every morning Achilles rose at dawn and dragged the body of Hector around the grave of Patroclus three times.

Achilles now routed the Trojans and drove them toward their city. Victory seemed certain, but Apollo guided an arrow from the bow of Paris and it pierced the heel of Achilles. It was his only vulnerable spot. When his mother, Thetis, dipped him in the River Styx as an infant to make him immortal, she held him by the heel and Styx did not touch it. Thetis now wept at his death.

ACHILLES' HEEL

Achilles, son of Peleus,
Fought in the battle of Troy.
He was an invincible warrior,
Those he fought he did destroy.

When just a tiny infant,
A dip in Styx he got.
Thetis held him by his heel,
His only vulnerable spot.

He slayed great Hector in battle,
And dragged his corpse around.
Apollo disguised as Paris,
Heel-shot him to the ground.

Before his death Achilles played an important role in the battle of Troy. When the Amazons came to the assistance of Troy, their warrior queen, Penthesilea, drove Achilles from the field on several occasions. Some say she once killed him but Zeus restored him to life through the persistent pleadings of Thetis. At last Achilles fell Penthesilea. As she lay dying Achilles fell in love with her. When Thersites, his fellow warrior, gouged out her eyes with his spear, Achilles killed him on the spot.

The Amazons were an amazing race of warrior women. Their queen was a daughter of Ares, the god of war. Her mother was Harmonia, goddess of Peace. Is it any wonder that she was confused?

The Amazons hated men but met with them once a year to propagate themselves. Following the mating they then killed their lovers and any male born of their union. They raised their girls to be warriors. When a girl reached the age of puberty, her right breast was cut off lest it impede the bow string.

THE AMAZONS

The Amazons were a warrior race
With contradictions in their stars.
Their mother was Harmonia,
Their father war-like Mars.

They were not husky, muscled men,
But very pretty maidens,
Who inspired almost godly awe
When with weapons they were laden.

They met with men but once a year
Just to propagate.
Then they killed their lovers
And the baby boys they hate.

But baby girls they raised with love,
Till puberty did show.
They then excised their right breast,
Lest it hinder spear and bow.

Penthesilea was their warrior queen.
She fought on the side of Troy.
She inspired the trepid Trojans,
As great Greeks she did destroy.

She sought out famed Achilles,
Before whom great Hector fell.
She hurled at him her deadly lance,
But she didn't ring the bell.

He hurled the lance of Cheiron,
Which never missed its mark.
It struck the irate Amazon,
And suddenly all was dark.

Achilles saw her beauty,
As she lay dying in the sand.
With bitter anguish in his heart,
He held her lovely hand.

Thersites mocked this warrior
For softness at a death.
Achilles in anger belted him.
And he breathed his final breath.

So long before the libbers
There were those who hated men.
They are a kind of Amazon,
Whom male breathing does offend.

The war was a stalemate. Neither side was winning and the Spartans longed for home. The war was now in its tenth year. Again the influence of the gods came into play as Athena now inspired Prylis, a son of Hermes, to suggest that the Greeks could enter the gates of Troy in a wooden horse. The artisan Epius volunteered to build it. Odysseus and other heroes hid within it as their fellow Greeks pretended to sail home.

Trojan scouts reported that the Greek camp was in ashes. The city rejoiced. The Greeks left Sinon bound near the horse to deceived the enemy. He informed the Trojans that the horse was a special gift from Athena. In celebration they took the horse into their city, over the protests of Cassandra, the prophetess who loudly warned them against this. That night as the Trojans slept after celebrating their day of victory, the Spartans slipped out of the horse, signaled their companions aboard the ships, opened the gates of Troy to admit them, and won the war.

CASSANDRA

The gift of prophesy
Apollo gave
To Cassandra
To win her heart.
But when she in turn
Rejected him,
He forced her
To depart.

A god could not
Take back a gift.
It would make him
A deceiver.
But he could, at least,
Annul its worth,
By making no one
Believe her.

And this is
Just what happened.
T'was a tragic thing,
Of course,
For Trojans
Wouldn't believe her,
When she warned
Of a wooden horse.

BEWARE OF GREEKS

The Spartans
In order to conquer Troy
Had to use
An unusual ploy.

Since they couldn't
Win by force,
Odysseus thought
Of the Wooden Horse.

Epeios made it
In a few short weeks
And hid inside
A lot of Greeks.

Agamemnon's army
Pretended flight
And sailed their ships
Just out of sight.

The horse was left
Upon the shore
And Sinon
With a plan in store.

He was bound
Both feet and hands
This was part
Of Spartan plans.

Advancing Trojans
Were amazed
While at the horse
They soundly gazed.

Sinon played his part
Quite well.
And this is what
He had to tell.

"The Greeks grew tired
And sailed for home
And he was left there
All alone.

They built the horse
To please Athene,
And then, dejected,
Fled the scene.

The Spartans made
The horse so tall
Lest it enter
The Trojan wall.

For Athena would favor
Any land
Where her beloved
Horse would stand."

Priest Laocoon
Was greatly miffed
And warned of Greeks
Who bore them gifts.

A serpent then
Came from the sea
Killing Laocoon
In agony.

Trojans took this
As a sign.
To move the horse
They set their mind.

They dragged it to
Their city wall.
It wouldn't fit.
It was too tall.

Their city wall
They soon knocked in
And proudly took
The horse within.

While Troy rejoiced
In wine that night,
The Spartan fleet
Retraced its flight.

Exhausted Trojans
Were asleep
As Spartans from
The horse did creep.

Trojans were slaughtered
The city burned,
Aided by
The fleet's return.

In every life
There's a Trojan Horse
That could surely change
Our plotted course.

We must weigh advice
Before we act.
Not everything
Is matter of fact.

Circumstances
We must sift,
Lest it be a Greek
That bears a gift.

Troy was lost,
Its treasures strewn,
Cause it didn't listen
To Laocoon.

PROBLEMS AND SOLUTIONS

Sometimes the gifts of the gods to men were contradictory in nature and resulted in the most confusing dilemmas. This is evidenced in the interesting tale told of a man name Amphitryon, the husband of Alcmene, the mother of Heracles by Zeus.

Alcmene demanded that her husband avenge the tragic deaths of her many brothers. Amphitryon agreed and sought the help of his friend, King Creon of Thebes.

Creon promised his help only if Amphitryon would rid the land of Thebes of the Teusmessian vixen, a fox that was uncatchable by decree of Zeus.

Procris had an infallible hound, divinely decreed to catch whatever it pursued. So Amphitryon borrowed this infallible hound from Procris to catch the uncatchable fox. It is the story of a dilemma.

It was while Amphitryon was on this chase that Zeus met with his wife, Alcmene, who bore him the great Heracles.

THE UNCATCHABLE FOX

Amphitryon was in a war
And needed lots of help.
Creon promised to give him aid,
If he'd catch a certain whelp.

It wasn't very nice of him,
For the whelp was the uncatchable fox.
No hunter who had ever lived
Could put him in a box.

But Amphitryon, himself, had tricks
That could force the fox aground.
For he had borrowed from Procris,
Laelaps, her infallible hound.

An uncatchable fox, an infallible hound,
Create quite an illusion.
An insoluble problem such as this
Would call for an insoluble solution.

Only Zeus could solve this mess,
The freaks that he had cloned.
He turned both frenzied fox and hound
Into a fox and hound of stone.

In our efforts to understand how human lives were often times pawns to divine intervention, we must not overlook Perseus, the son of Zeus and Danae.

Acrisius was married to Aganippe. Danae was their daughter. He had no son and consulted an oracle on what he must do to beget a male heir. The oracle responded: "You will have no son and your grandson will kill you."

To prevent a grandson Acrisius imprisoned Danae in the castle tower. Bars were not obstacles to Zeus. He descended upon Danae and she begot a son named Perseus. In fear and desperation Acrisius put his daughter and grandson in a wooden box and cast it into the sea.

It drifted toward the Island of Seriphos where a fisherman named Dictys discovered it. Perseus and Danae were welcomed to this new country by King Polydectes. When Perseus grew up the king wanted to marry Danae. She refused the queenship offered her, and Perseus was an obstacle to the king's taking her by force. To rid himself of Perseus the king sent him on a royal mission to cut off the head of Medusa. Athena, a long time enemy of the gorgon Medusa, aided Perseus and warned him never to look at Medusa's head. If he did so, he would be turned to stone.

Hermes gave him winged sandals to fly at great speeds and a sickle to accomplish his task. When the dangerous deed was done he set out for home.

On his return he saved Andromeda from a sea monster and claimed her for his wife. He returned to the Island of Seriphos in time to save his mother from Polydectes whom he also turned to stone.

PERSEUS

The plot of Polydectes,
Whose heart for Danae bled,
Sent Perseus in hot pursuit
Of Medusa's head.

With gifts from gods
He quickly flew,
And cut the Gorgon
Right in two.

The head he carried in a bag,
For it was widely known,
That those who look upon it,
Would be turned to stone.

He rescued Andromeda,
From denizens of deep,
Before her royal parents
Who were too alarmed to weep.

He claimed her
For his lovely bride
While father and mother
Looked on with pride.

To her uncle Phineus
She had been engaged
He now shows up quite boldly
And is thoroughly enraged.

But Perseus had a bag of tricks
That turned enemies into stone.
So Perseus, our great hero, fled
With Andromeda all alone.

And when he came to Seriphos
Polydectes got his due.
For bothering dear Danae
He was made a stone statue.

There was a time in which angry gods destroyed the entire earth in punishment for the wickedness of men. Only the pious Deucalion and his wife Pyrra were spared by the gods. They were warned to build an ark to escape the wrath of the gods who would flood the earth.

When the waters later subsided, they piously prayed to the gods to replenish the earth. They were told to throw the bones of Mother Earth over their shoulders. They were puzzled at first, but soon realized the bones of Mother Earth were stones.

Men rose from the stones thrown by Deucalion. Women rose from the stones cast by Pyrra.

THE FLOOD

The gods were angered by ungrateful men,
And in punishment sent a flood,
A rather neat way to destroy the earth,
Cause it doesn't shed much blood.

The waters rose to Parnassus,
Too deep for man to wade.
Deucalion and Pyrrha were saved
In a little ark they made.

They disembarked in safety,
Offering sacrifice to Zeus.
They prayed at the shrine of Themis,
Beside the river Cephissus.

They pleaded humbly to the gods
That mankind they'd renew.
Told throw the bones of Mother Earth,
Children rose from the stones they threw.

THE WHY OF SEASONS

Ceres or Demeter was the goddess of the harvest. She was the sister of Zeus and by him begot Persephone, the pride and joy of her life. As Ceres went about busily planting the fields, Persephone joyfully assisted her.

One day Pluto, the god of the under world, stealthily kidnaped Persephone and carried her off to Hades to be his queen. Saddened at her loss, Ceres refused to plant the fields until Zeus would demand the return of the child. Soon famine extended to the very borders of the earth and Zeus was forced to act. He ordered Hades to return Persephone to her mother. Pluto had a plan to circumvent the command of Zeus. The Fates had decreed that anyone who had eaten in Hades must remain there forever. Even the gods are bound by the enduring decrees of Fate.

As Persephone made her way back to earth, Pluto offered her a pomegranate. She tasted it but did not swallow it because its taste was too bitter. But because of this taste she must spend some time in Hades to fulfill the demands of the Fates. Half of her time she spends on earth with her mother. The other half she spends with Hades. Only when Persephone is with her will Ceres plant the fields. When she winters in Hades, Ceres permits nothing to grow.

PERSEPHONE

When Ceres
Lost her daughter,
Over all the earth
She sought her.

She didn't know
That Hades
Stole Persephone
From her daisies.

She refused
To plant her fields,
Till Hades
Her daughter yields.

Famine spread
Throughout the land.
Zeus must take
This thing in hand.

Hermes he sends
To the netherworld
To return the child
To this world.

Zeus took his decree
For granted,
But saw not
Pomegranate.

So a pact was made
With Hades' King.
She would return
With every spring.

Zeus promised
He would send her
Back to Hades
Every winter.

So we have
The why of seasons.
Greek myths give us
The reasons.

Flowers when Persephone
Walks the earth.
But when in Hades,
Only dearth.

CENTAURS

Centaurs were a rare race of creatures that were half man and half horse. Their lower body was that of a horse. From the neck up they were men.

Some were mean and rascally as was Nessus, the Centaur that stole the wife of Heracles. Some Centaurs were kind, compassionate, and brave. Such a one was Cheiron. He was brilliant of mind and became the tutor of the greatest heroes of Greece. Even gods were entrusted to his care. It was he who taught Asclepius the art of healing, the practice of which, got the lad into all sorts of trouble with the gods.

It was Cheiron's willingness to die in his place that freed the great Prometheus from the rock.

CHEIRON

Cheiron was a Centaur
Half man and half a horse.
Immortalized he taught the gods
And they always aced his course.

He even taught Asclepius
The art of restoring life,
A deed he did for Glaucus,
Son of Minos and his wife.

Such miracles angered Hades,
The reason, of course, you know.
When people do not enter death,
His kingdom doesn't grow.

THE THORN OF THEBES

When Oedipus resigned his reign over Thebes, his sons, Eteocles and Polynices, were to share its rule, each in alternating years. At the end of the first year Eteocles refused to step down and sent his brother into exile.

After a time, Polynices and Tydeus, both fugitives from their homeland, married the daughters of Adrastus king of Argos. He promised to right the wrong done to his sons-in-law.

He first organized seven armies to advance against Thebes. He was warned against doing so by Amphiaraus, a wise soothsayer, who had married Eriphyle, the sister of Adrastus. The seer foresaw total defeat for the men of Argos.

Amphiaraus and Adrastus never saw eye to eye, but when Adrastus gave him his sister (Eriphyle) in marriage, he solemnly swore that in all future disagreements with Adrastus he would follow the will of Eriphyle. Knowing this, Polynices bribed Eriphyle with the necklace that Aphrodite gave to Harmonia when she married Cadmus. It was her decision that sent Amphiaraus to the death he foretold.

The Argives were badly defeated at Thebes. Eteocles and Polynices killed each other in single combat. The defenders of Thebes slaughtered the armies of Argos. Only Adrastus survived and escaped on his winged horse, Arion.

Creon, the uncle of Eteocles and Polynices and brother-in-law of Oedipus, became the king. He forbid the burial of Polynices, vengeance for his own son's death, Menoeceus, who was the required sacrifice for victory.

Antigone, sister of the fallen brothers, could not bear to see Polynices unattended. She buried him and became the victim of her uncles insane anger, even though she was engaged to marry his son, Haemon.

The irrational tragedies that resulted from Creon's vengeance unfold in the story of the Seven Against Thebes.

Ten years later the descendants of the fallen heroes under the leadership of Alcmaeon avenged their fathers. The eight descendants were called Epigoni. Alcmaeon was the son of Amphiaraus who foretold defeat but was tricked into battle by the greed of his wife. The young Alcmaeon promised his father to settle accounts with his mother if his predictions came true.

Following the victory, the Epigoni took Manto, daughter of Tiresias, to Delphi were she became a priestess to Apollo. Alcmaeon returned home and killed his mother.

SEVEN AGAINST THEBES

King Adrastus had two daughters
And an oracle spoke this lore.
One would marry a lion;
The other would marry a bore.

Not wanting cubs for royal heirs,
The king fretted quite a bit.
He sought suitors for his daughters,
But they never made a hit.

One night he heard a struggle
Outside his castle gate.
Two fugitives had met there
By decree, perhaps, of Fate.

Tydeus and Polynices
Fought before his door.
On one shield was stamped a lion,
On the other was marked a boar.

Soon Argia and Deiphyle
Were to these visitors wed,
But they and other heroes
At Thebes would soon be dead.

Oedipus left his Thebian throne
For both his sons to share.
But Eteocles grabbed it all.
And that really wasn't fair.

So the King of Argos agreed to help
Polynices regain his throne,
Which his brother Eteocles
Took as his very own.

The Argives set out for Thebes,
Adrastus at their head.
Seven armies altogether,
Which each a hero led.

Argives were at the walls of Thebes
So Thebians planned defense.
Eteocles and Uncle Creon knew
Their problems were immense.

Creon consulted Tiresias,
A seer with no eyes.
He predicted victory, only if
Someone beloved dies.

Tiresias said that Thebes would win
But only at a price.
The youngest descendant of Cadmus
Must be offered in sacrifice.

That youngest was Menoeceus,
Creon's youngest son.
Creon told him he must flee
Ere such a deed was done.

But Menoeceus was proud to die
To save Thebes, his fatherland.
So he climbed a top the city walls.
And died at his own hand.

Polynices hurled a challenge
For single combat with his brother.
Eteocles gladly accepted it
And each did kill the other.

Then Thebians swarmed in battle
And slayed Argives without remorse.
Adrastus, their king, alone was left,
He fled on Arion, his winged horse.

Creon who became the king
Buried Eteocles in royal plot.
He decreed for Polynices,
"In the field let him rot."

But Antigone, his sister,
Could not let her brother lie.
She sneaked out and buried him
And Creon hit the sky.

He ordered her interred alive
In a sealed cave.
She would gradually starve to death
And it would be her grave.

What a way to treat a niece,
Engaged to wed his son!
But despite the pleas of Haemon
The commanded deed was done.

Haemon, enraged, rolled back the stone
To release his future wife.
But when he looked inside the cave
She had taken her own life.

In despair she'd hanged herself.
Haemon cut her down,
Then thrust a knife into his throat
And died upon the ground.

Meantime Creon changed his mind
Warned to do so by the seer.
He hurried off unto the cave
Where he came at last to free her.

He saw Angtigone in Haemon's arms,
Both of them quite dead.
The saddened father realized
In death they had been wed.

With heavy heart he went back home,
There to tell his wife.
But Eurydice knew from messengers
And in grief had taken her life.

ORIGIN OF THE NEMEAN GAMES

Adrastus led his armies
To Thebes they bravely marched.
But in the land of Nemea
They suddenly grew parched.

They saw a woman with a child
As they searched for water.
It was beautiful Hypsipyle,
The King of Lemnos' daughter.

She had been sold as a slave
To Lycurgus, Nemea's king.
She served as royal nursemaid,
Prince Opheltes neath her wing.

She led them to a secret spring
That flowed with rushing water.
King Adrastus and his men
Were indebted to Thaos' daughter.

But first this gentle woman
Laid Opheltes on soft grass.
And when the thirsty crowd returned.
He'd been eaten by an asp.

Grieving Hypsipyle
Found his infant bones picked bare
And the sated serpent
Resting in its lair.

Hippomedon hurled his spear
And doused the serpent's flames.
In memory of Opheltes
They founded Nemean Games.

Eurydice, Lycurgus' wife,
Vowed death to careless nurse.
But sons long searching, found her
And spared her from this curse.

THE EPIGONI

Ten years after defeat at Thebes,
Where their fathers fell,
The sons of fallen heroes
Attacked Thebes' citadel.

They were called the Epigoni
And they numbered eight.
They'd soon avenge their fathers
This would be their fate.

Alcmaeon was their leader,
Amphiaraus' son.
He could kill his mother
After the battle's won.

They arrived at the walls of Thebes.
Its citizens were distraught.
The sound advise of Tiresias
By them was quickly sought.

He advised them flee their town,
While heralds offered peace.
So in darkness of the night
They fled with their valise.

Tiresias died in the flight,
He was now a hundred years old.
His daughter Manto stayed in Thebes,
For she was rather bold.

Conquerors entered abandoned Thebes,
Vowing Apollo what they found,
Their find was gifted Manto,
A seer of great renown.

The victors took her to Delphi
To perform Apollo's rites,
A consecrated priestess,
Her father's satellite.

In her temple she taught an old man,
A singer, poet, and roamer.
He had come from Maeonia
And became the gifted Homer.

Good from evil can always come
As evil can come from good.
It's all a matter of point of view
And how it's understood.

Vengeance that seethed for many years
Certainly is no misnomer.
It never can be justified,
But it gave the world Homer.

CADMUS' FAMILY CURSE

Cadmus was Phoencian,
A grandson of Poseidon
He gave the world the alphabet
That its horizons widen.

The whims of gods controlled his life
In each and every phase.
There was no man who ever lived
Who saw more bitter days.

Europa was his sister
With whom Zeus did sojourn
Cadmus, sent to find her,
Never did return.

Gods told him follow a certain cow
And stop where that cow feeds,
Then build a city on the spot
And name that city Thebes.

A serpent son of Ares
Suddenly killed his men.
Cadmus in anger killed it
And Ares did offend.

Athena told him sow the teeth
Of the dragon that was dead.
From those teeth fierce warriors came
That Cadmus later led.

He married sweet Harmonia.
Vulcan's necklace was her present.
Muses sang their wedding song,
Olympians made their presence.

Soon tragedies befell them
As Ares sought revenge,
Violence of every sort
Till dead serpent was avenged.

For Cadmus and Harmonia
This was more than they could bear.
They fled from their beloved Thebes
As Cadmus offered up a prayer.

"If serpents are so blessed by gods
That their killings cause such grief,
Let me become a serpent
So I can find relief."

No sooner had he said this
Than skin grew into scale.
His feet and arms then disappeared
As they became his tail.

Harmonia, when she saw this,
A similar prayer did make
And slithered off with Cadmus
When she, too, became a snake.

So watch the things you pray for,
Especially when discouraged.
You could make an asp of yourself,
Mistaking cowardice for courage.

SOME FINAL STORIES

NAMING A CITY

A town grew up in Attica
Which one day would win fame.
Poseidon and lovely Athena
Wished it to bear their name.

To avoid a bitter quarrel,
The Olympians held a test.
Each would give a generous gift
And their name, if it were best.

Poseidon struck his trident
And hit the earth with force.
And to the awe of all the gods
Sprang forth a beautiful horse.

Athena touched her spear to ground,
And gods wondered what would be.
Then slowly from the soil came
The dark black olive tree.

The gods with future vision saw
The blessing this would bring.
Its harvest and its industry
Would make the city king.

So Athena won the contest,
A tribute to her wits.
Athens got its olives;
Poseidon got the pits.

LETHE, RIVER OF FORGETFULNESS

When Atropos cuts
Our strings of life
With dreaded
Silver shears.
We are given
Funeral rites
Then Mercury
Appears.

He transports us
To Hades realm
Where we are met
By Charon
Who ferries us
Cross River Styx
To a kingdom
That's quite barren.

A River
Of Forgetfulness
Flows through
This land of Shades.
We stoop and drink
From Lethe's spring
And memory
Soon fades.

Its magic waters
Are consumed
To forget the life
We're leaving.
The cares that grieved us
While we lived
We'll be no longer
Grieving.

All thoughts of earth
Are washed away
And how
We suffered there.
The things that pained us
While we lived
We need
No longer bear.

But there's a price
We have to pay
To forget
Unpleasant thought.
For joys
As well as sorrows
Will also come
To naught.

We will forget
Past sufferings,
Certainly,
This is true.
But remember, too,
We will forget
All the joys
We knew.

There'll be no thought
Of failures past
Or those despised
Above.
But there'll be no thought
Of by-gone friends
Or those
We truly love.

So before you drink,
Consider well
All the
Consequences.
What you'll gain
And what you'll lose
Before you burn
Your fences.

THE GREAT GOD PAN

Pan was quite an ugly god
Who looked much like a goat,
With goat like feet and horns on head
And hair upon his throat.

Chasing after Arcadian nymphs
He always was rejected,
But this happy-go-lucky ugly god
Never became dejected.

He pursued poor Syrinx, a lovely nymph,
But he wasn't at all her type.
She turned herself into a reed,
Which Pan picked for his pan-pipe.

He loved his nap each afternoon,
For he really was quite lazy.
And if awakened by passerby
He suddenly went crazy.

He shrieked his irritation
With a cry that was quite frantic.
All who heard were struck with fear,
A fear now known as panic.

Pan was the only god to die
As the sailor, Thaumas, said.
In fact, he shouted to the world:
"The great god Pan is dead."

CONCLUSION

The Greeks no longer have their gods.
Long ago they ceased to be.
But they live on in the minds of men.
And this shall always be.

So study all you can of them,
And of all the things they did.
Their stories still bring joy to us,
Fairy tales for grown up kids.